FROM
SUFFRAGETTE
TO FASCIST

FROM
SUFFRAGETTE
TO FASCIST

THE MANY LIVES OF
MARY SOPHIA ALLEN

NINA BOYD

The
History
Press

First published 2013

The History Press
The Mill, Brimscombe Port
Stroud, Gloucestershire, GL5 2QG
www.thehistorypress.co.uk

British Library Cataloguing in Publication Data.
A catalogue record for this book is available from the British Library.

ISBN 978 0 7524 8917 9

Typesetting and origination by The History Press
Printed in Great Britain

CONTENTS

PREFACE

I first came across Mary Sophia Allen on a rainy day in Ripon, North Yorkshire, in 2001. Caught by a sudden downpour I took refuge in the nearby Prison and Police Museum. In a room full of helmets, whistles, handcuffs, police notebooks, dominated by a waxwork sergeant, the most interesting item was a postcard in a rack.

I took my postcard home and made a quick internet search of its subject. Mary Allen was a mystery: a fighter for women's rights and an unsung hero of policing, who transformed herself into a political virago.

She was difficult to research, having been unmarried and childless; but distant relatives all over the world dug out memories and photographs. I am indebted to them all.

I cannot hope to rescue the reputation that Mary lost by her own wilfulness and folly. But I do believe that this opinionated, infuriating woman should not be entirely forgotten.

ACKNOWLEDGEMENTS

My thanks to the descendants of Mary's siblings: Penny Gill and Rosemary Frouws in South Africa, and Margaret Bateman in Ireland; and to Vicky Tagart, who provided copies of family letters.

Also to the people at various organisations who answered requests for information, including The League of Women Voters, Buffalo, Niagara; Lynda James, Bereavement Services Advisor, Croydon; and the Public Record Office; and to the generous people who have given me additional information, including Pat Benham, Val Jackson, Joan Lock and Paul Ashdown.

And to those who read early attempts at a manuscript: Jill Liddington, Carola Luther and Andrew Biswell; Alan Henness, who helped me with my website; and my own supportive family, particularly John Bosley, Jacqueline Bosley, Maria Fernandez, Lynda Hulou, and Eleanor, Bill and Tom Boddington.

LIST OF ABBREVIATIONS

ASL	Artists' Suffrage League
BJN	British Journal of Nursing
CLAC	Criminal Law Amendment Committee
DORA	Defence of the Realm Act
FANY	First Aid Nursing Yeomanry
GWR	Great Western Railway
ILP	Independent Labour Party
IRA	Irish Republican Army
MWPP	Metropolitan Women Police Patrols
NUWSS	National Union of Women's Suffrage Societies
NUWW	National Union of Women Workers
NVA	National Vigilance Association
PRO	Public Record Office
WAS	Women's Auxiliary Service
WFL	Women's Freedom League
WPP	Women Police Patrols
WPS	Women's Police Service
WPV	Women Police Volunteers
WSPU	Women's Social and Political Union
WVP	Women Voluntary Patrols

PROLOGUE

In 1915, Mary Allen and her lover, Margaret Damer Dawson, had their hair cropped and posed for a photographer. They wore the uniforms they had designed for themselves as leaders of a newly formed women's police service: military-style peaked caps, long greatcoats, tightly knotted ties and highly polished jackboots.

They are tall women, standing side by side in a formal pose, their feet positioned awkwardly at right angles. They take their roles as pioneer policewomen seriously; but at the same time, the nature of their relationship is apparent from the way they stand half-turned towards one another, the fingers of their white gloves intertwined. There is a hint of a smile on Mary's face.

They had known each other for only a few months, but Margaret, who had no reason to know that she would only live another five years, had already made a will, leaving her substantial fortune to Mary.

In the seven years since she had been banished from her father's comfortable home, Mary had observed the working of the law from all sides: as a suffragette she had been imprisoned three times and forcibly fed while on hunger strike; later she accompanied a deputation of members of Parliament on an inspection of conditions in Holloway Jail; and she became second-in-command to Margaret Damer Dawson in the first women's police service. She took over as commandant of the Women's Police Service after the death of Margaret.

Mary was a constant irritant to the Metropolitan Police Force which has effectively erased her from their history of women's policing. She became well known in all corners of the world as the leading British policewoman, while the authorities at home no longer recognised her as *any* sort of policewoman. Curiously, she was asked in 1923 to advise the government on policing the post-First World War British occupation of Germany, long after she had been instructed by the same government to disband her police force.

After a meeting with Hitler, Mary embraced fascism and supported Oswald Mosley. She came close to being interned for her political activities in the 1940s. It may be that only her growing eccentricity saved her from detention.

Mary Allen's story is extraordinary. She was a woman of whom it would be impossible for any liberal-minded reader to approve, but at the same time she inspired deep affection and loyalty from friends and family throughout her long and eventful life.

I

A Benevolent
Dictatorship

We tend to remember the house we grew up in as being much bigger than
it actually was; but Mary Allen's childhood home was certainly substantial by modern standards. She was part of a household of two parents, ten
children, and assorted nannies, governesses and servants, and they were not
cramped for space:

> As we grew older, boys and girls rode a velocipede around the garden paths,
> and on rainy days (forbidden joy!) even along the corridors. A velocipede!
> The name itself was an enchantment. Can any later invention provide a
> more fascinating suggestion of speed produced by short gyrating legs?[1]

Little is known of Mary's childhood. She was always reticent about the
details of her private life, in marked contrast with her partiality to self-
advertisement in the public sphere. In her first volume of autobiography,
The Pioneer Policewoman, she claims that she was 'a very delicate child, educated almost entirely at home, and denied all the training in outdoor sports
of the robust modern girl. Increased mental activity may possibly have been
the result of this intolerable physical restraint.'[2] Yet it was a busy, active childhood, fondly remembered fifty years later in *A Woman at the Cross Roads*,
when Victorian values and the virtues of discipline and hard work had been
replaced by what Mary perceived as dangerous libertarianism. 'We invented
games, made things, carpentered, jig-sawed, dug in the garden.' (p.15) There
were outings to a pantomime at Christmas, and three or four visits a year to
the theatre, 'either as a birthday treat or as a reward for good conduct'. (p.30)
She describes a series of governesses, of varying quality and ability, but all
respected and obeyed by their charges.

We might expect a childhood as apparently happy as Mary Allen's to be
recounted in more detail by a woman who wrote three autobiographies;

but in none of them does she even tell us the first names of her brothers and sisters, or recall anecdotes from her earliest years. All she tells us is that her large family was not unusual, and that nannies were important figures, more present in the children's lives than their parents:

> From the age of two, or even earlier, we recognised a benevolent dic-
> tatorship – a discipline firm but not harsh (in spite of novels that make
> the exceptional seem the usual state of affairs). It was a brave child who
> would dare defy Nannie! ... In looking back, it seems to me that we
> were very rarely punished. Not to be permitted to go down-stairs to
> join our parents in the real dining-room, to say good night, was a bitter
> humiliation. (pp.15–16)

Although Mary was educated mostly at home by governesses, she attended Princess Helena College, Ealing, when her father's work took the family to London. The Princess Helena College was established in 1820 as one of England's first academic schools for girls, founded for the daughters of officers who had served in the Napoleonic Wars, and the daughters of Anglican clergy. Mary gained a good education there judging by her literary output. Although her style is sometimes florid, she writes well, and displays a thorough knowledge of history. Mary is remembered in the annals of the college:

> Another well-known figure in public life, Miss Mary Allen, the thrice-
> gaoled suffragette, returned to the College and talked to the girls about
> the Women's Police, which she and a friend had launched. Sixty years
> later, in 1983, Marjory Lucas [a pupil in 1923] had still not forgotten the
> extraordinary visitor who 'appeared large and important' in uniform,
> hatted, 'and sort of marched about'. But Miss Allen had yet to espouse the
> Fascist cause.[3]

Mary Sophia Allen was born on 12 March 1878 at 2 Marlborough Terrace in Roath, a suburb of Cardiff, not far from the divisional office of the Great Western Railway in St Mary Street, where her father was Railway Superintendent. Three years later, the family moved to a larger terraced house on four floors in nearby Oakfield Street.

Thomas Isaac Allen, Mary's father, had entered the railway service when he was 15 years old, as a junior clerk. It was a boom time for ambitious young men, and he worked his way up to the position of Chief Superintendent of the Great Western Railway. He was much respected by his peers as a talented engineer, responsible for instituting a number of improvements in the GWR, including restaurant cars, better conditions for third-class passengers, steam heating of trains, and accelerated express services. His status within the GWR hierarchy is indicated by the fact that he represented the company on royal occasions. At the funeral of Queen Victoria in 1901, he accompanied the royal train from Paddington and, as one of the organisers of the event, he received a commemorative medal. The following year, he was photographed wearing a uniform specially designed for him for the Coronation of Edward VII. Thomas was then a fine-looking man in his early sixties, sporting a full white beard and luxuriant moustache.

In the notice of his retirement in the *Great Western Railway Magazine*, Thomas Allen is said to have filled the position of superintendent of the line 'with great advantage to the company and much credit to himself … Mr Allen has always been keenly alive to the interests of the company, and also ever mindful of the welfare of the staff, with whom he is deservedly popular.'[4]

Thomas Allen's position gave his family privileged access to railway travel, at home and abroad. His daughters travelled a great deal, and went to finishing school in Switzerland, and took music lessons in Germany.[5] 'When they travelled in England they had a special coach hitched on to the train they were travelling by. In Switzerland and France they were always met by railway officials who smoothed their paths.'[6] Thomas died aged 72 years old in Brighton on 20 December 1911, having made a will three weeks earlier leaving everything to his wife. The net value of his estate was £1,987 18s 11d; the equivalent in 2012 of approximately £164,000.

Mary's mother, Margaret Sophia Carlyle, came from a distinguished family, the Carlyles of Dumfries. She brought money and social cachet to the marriage. Her father was the Reverend Benjamin Fearnley Carlyle, vicar of Cam in Gloucestershire, who compiled a number of books of hymns and psalms. Margaret had two younger sisters, Anne and Dorothy, and an older brother, James, who was the father of another Benjamin Fearnley Carlyle, an eccentric charismatic character, who became known as Dom Aelred.

Margaret, Mary's mother, went regularly and in secret to London to visit Mary after she was banished from the family home. She made her home in London after Thomas died. One of her granddaughters remembered:

We used to go from Edinburgh to London to Putney where she had a flat, to stay with her for holidays. I remember once we decided on the spur of the moment to go to Brussels to see Auntie Elsie who lived there and we gave grandmother ten minutes to get ready. When we were on the steamer we noticed that she had one black shoe on and one brown one and when we told her she said 'That's allright, nobody looks at an old lady like me' and was quite unconcerned.[7]

Margaret Allen died in London in 1933.

Dom Aelred exerted considerable influence on his female cousins, one of whom, as we shall see, became a nun. Aelred began his professional life as a medical student at St Bartholomew's Hospital, London, but he gave up medicine in order to become an Anglican Benedictine oblate. He took the name Aelred and founded the Benedictine community which, in 1906, settled on Caldey Island off the south-west coast of Wales:

> Benjamin (Aelred) Carlyle, who had been fascinated by the monastic life since the age of fifteen, when he had founded a secret religious brotherhood at his public school … was a man of dynamic personality, hypnotic eyes, and extraordinary imagination. In 1906 his community made its permanent home on Caldey Island, off the coast of south Wales (outside Anglican diocesan jurisdiction), where, largely on borrowed money, he built a splendidly furnished monastery in a fanciful style of architecture. The life of this enclosed Benedictine community centred upon an ornate chapel where the thirty or so tonsured and cowled monks sang the monastic offices and celebrated Mass in Latin according to the Roman rite. As there was nothing like it anywhere else in the Church of England the island abbey inevitably became a resort for ecclesiastical sightseers, and many young men were drawn to join the community out of personal affection for Carlyle. The self-styled Lord Abbot of Caldey introduced practices into the life of his monastery which many outsiders, accustomed to the austere atmosphere of the existing Anglican men's communities, found disconcerting … during the summer months they regularly went sea-bathing in the nude. Nor did Carlyle make any secret of his liking for charming young men.[8]

Aelred's biographer, a former member of the Caldey Island community, remarked that spiritual friendships were 'not discouraged'.[9] In 1913 Aelred and a number of his monks renounced the Anglican Church and were received into the Roman Catholic Church. He spent some years work-ing in the Canadian mission fields, but returned to his community and moved to Prinknash near Gloucester, where he is honoured as the founder of the present Benedictine community. He died in 1955, and is buried at Prinknash Abbey.[10]

Mary's parents, Thomas and Margaret, had ten children, five girls and five boys, all but the youngest born in Cardiff. Bunty Martin, the daughter of their youngest daughter, Christine, said perhaps unfairly that 'the girls of that family were the "go getters". The brothers were very dull.'[11]

Thomas Fearnley Allen, Mary's eldest brother, who bore a strong resem-blance to his father, became an engineer, and settled in Argentina, where in 1885 he was appointed by the directors of the Buenos Aires and Rosario Railway as their Locomotive and Carriage Engineer and placed in charge of the shops at Campana. He married Ann Irving Lawrie, a descendant of one of the first Scottish settlers to arrive in the Argentine. They had three sons and a daughter. Some members of this branch of the family are still living in Argentina.

The second of Mary's siblings, Henry Bevill, died when he was 11 months old. Her third brother, Arthur Denys Allen, known as Denys, 'invented things', according to his niece. 'I met him once and he took us for a ride in his Model T Ford.'[12] Another brother, Herbert, who became a master mari-ner, was killed in the First World War. Edward, the youngest of the Allen children, was born when the family had moved to Ealing.

The five Allen girls were energetic and outgoing. The eldest, Margaret Annie, was always known as Dolly. She is the person Mary refers to in *The Pioneer Policewoman* and *Lady in Blue* as 'my sister, Mrs Hampton'. Dolly was involved with Mary in the setting up of the Women Police Volunteers (later renamed the Women Police Service), and was the only member of that service eventually employed by the Metropolitan Police, working at Richmond as an Inspector and probation officer. She had a daughter, Marjorie, and a son, called Wilfred after his father. Wilfred was a Polar explorer and pilot. He and his companions on a Greenland expedition were the first explorers ever to be awarded Polar Medals with both Arctic and Antarctic silver bars. Dolly was, like her sisters, attracted to religion, and she became a Christian Science practitioner.

Mary Sophia was the second daughter, and she was followed by Elsie, who married Herbert Joseph Cotton, a captain in the Indian Army. In 1911,

Elsie and her daughter were living with her parents in Wraysbury, outside London, but her husband was absent, serving overseas. He died in Baghdad on 22 May 1916, having been taken prisoner by the Turks after the siege of Kut-al-Amara. Major Cotton was seriously ill with enteric fever when Kut surrendered at the end of April. Along with other sick officers, he was put on a steamer and sent up the river to Baghdad, a journey which took ten days. He died a few days after their arrival in Baghdad, and was buried in the Christian cemetery there. The cemetery has recently been destroyed in conflict. His possessions, apart from a few personal items kept back for his wife, were sold by auction in the cavalry barracks.[13] Elsie remarried and lived for the rest of her life in Belgium.

Janet and Christine, Mary's younger sisters, became involved in a strange and celebrated adventure. Both were inclined to the mystical, seeing visions and, in Christine's case, practising automatic writing. They were two of the 'three maidens' who assisted Wellesley Tudor Pole in 1906 in his quest for the Holy Grail. (This story is told in Patrick Benham's *The Avalonians;*[14] and Gerry Fenge's *The Two Worlds of Wellesley Tudor Pole.*[15])

In 1885 J.A. Goodchild, a doctor with a winter practice in Italy, bought an old blue glass bowl from a tailor in Bordighera. Goodchild felt it might be the Holy Grail and, twelve years after buying the bowl, he had a psychic experience in which he was told to take it (he now called it 'The Cup') to Bride's Hill at Glastonbury, where he hid it in a hollow under a stone in the waters of a well, confident that it would be found and understood as a holy relic. Several years passed, and Dr Goodchild began to wonder if he should do something to expedite the finding of 'The Cup'. On one of his annual pilgrimages to the well, he found a note tied to a bush, left there by Kitty Tudor Pole, the sister of Wellesley Tudor Pole (a man he had already met), and he visited her at her home in Bristol.

Kitty's friends, Janet and Christine Allen, and her brother, Wellesley, became involved in the affair. After a series of visions, Wellesley Tudor Pole became convinced that 'something wonderful, remarkable, even Grail-like, was to be found at Glastonbury', and that three maidens were needed to help him find it. Kitty, Janet and Christine Allen were willing volunteers. They had first met when Christine was 17. 'The Allen girls were always considered beauties, and much in demand at parties, tall, slender and graceful, with golden hair and blue eyes.'[16]

Despite their fragile beauty, Wellesley Tudor Pole had no qualms about sending them to dig in 3ft of mud at Glastonbury, where they found 'The Cup', which became an object of reverence, kept in a room at Wellesley Tudor Pole's house in Royal York Crescent, Clifton, Bristol. The room was designated the Oratory, and vigils were held there. Janet was particularly eager to spend hours in the Oratory: 'We took three hours there at a time and six hours off night and day. It was rather sleepy work sometimes. At twelve every day, or rather 11.40, we had a special service, also smaller services at three and seven.' It is alleged that baptisms and marriages were conducted in the Oratory, as well as a form of communion. According to Patrick Benham, Annie Kenney and Emmeline Pethick-Lawrence, two of the suffragists with whom Mary worked closely, visited the Oratory.[17]

Even Mary's father, Thomas Isaac Allen, was caught up in these events, 'arriving at the Oratory one morning "in rather a way", to tell his two daughters that "he had dreamt of fire" and must warn them, especially Christine, "the younger one", whose volatile nature was capable of attracting mishap'.[18]

Janet and Christine devoted much time to their research, visiting Rome and Iona together to investigate links between the Celtic and Roman churches; and Janet continued to correspond with Goodchild with whom she shared an interest in the theory that the Church of Rome was founded by a woman, and a belief in the power of gematria (the interpretation of Scripture through assigning numerical values to alphabetical letters).

This account shows that some members of Mary Allen's family – including her father – were highly suggestible; but we should remember that many prominent and influential members of society dabbled in spiritualism and the occult at this time; some of them, including Sir Arthur Conan Doyle, taking supernatural beliefs extremely seriously. Sir William Crookes was a friend of the Allen family. He was both an eminent scientist – the discoverer of the metal thallium, who also refined methods of electric lighting – and a practising spiritist. He was an active member of the Society for Psychical Research, which investigated mediums and other psychic phenomena.

The events at Glastonbury were reported with a degree of scepticism by the *Daily Express* on 26 July 1907:

> Being unable to spare time from his business to go to Glastonbury, Mr Tudor Pole sent his sister and two other ladies, one of whom is a 'clairvoyante', to the spot. Whatever the cup may be, the story has succeeded in stirring the greatest interest in the minds of men and women of distinction.

Wellesley Tudor Pole wrote a letter to the *Daily Express* the following day, in which he stated with breathtaking pomposity that:

> The question of credulity or incredulity on the part of the public is a matter of absolute indifference to me, and I should like this known. Proof

will be forthcoming in due course as the result of present research and in the interim the opinion of the world is valueless.

Janet was deeply interested in religion, spending much of her time in various retreats and pursuing the question of the ordination of women. In 1920, she was received into the Catholic Church at Westminster Cathedral, taking the names Margaret Brigid. The following year, she entered the enclosed Benedictine community at Stanbrook Abbey, Worcestershire, as a novice. 'She is a convert, and about 40, and has always been very delicate, but a most sincere disposition, full of zeal.' She made her solemn, perpetual vows on 24 June 1926: 'Most of her family were present, although they declared they would never see her again … Commandant Allen, DBC [*sic*], sister of Sr. Brigid, was here.'[19] Nuns at Stanbrook took the title 'Dame' once they had made solemn, perpetual vows. Dame Brigid continued her researches at Stanbrook, and kept in touch by letter with Kitty Tudor Pole. Her niece, Bunty Martin, wrote:

> The last time I saw her was when she came to stay with us in Edinburgh in 1926 just prior to her taking final vows … I never saw Auntie Janet again but wrote to her frequently and received many letters from her telling us of the life she led and the funny things that happened to her – like the day she broke her chamber pot and had to take the pieces and lay them on the altar in the Chapel and ask God's forgiveness for her carelessness. She said she felt rather foolish … She had a lovely sense of humour. Then we heard that she had cancer of the spine and was lying in a cold little cell, so we sent her a hotwater bottle and a bedjacket and we hoped that she would have been allowed to use them. We loved her very much.[20]

Those of her immediate family who visited Janet at Stanbrook found it 'a most distressing occurrence going to see Auntie Janet who was behind bars, most upsetting it was'.[21] Janet died in 1945.

Christine Allen, Mary's youngest sister, was remembered by her daughter, Bunty Martin. Christine, 'led quite an adventurous life for a girl of her time … My mother, Kitty [Tudor Pole] and Janet were very earnest young ladies with a Mission in life and my mother kept searching for the Truth until the day she died.'[22] In 1911, the year of Thomas Allen's death, Christine moved to Edinburgh. She married the artist John Duncan, a man some twenty years her senior, in the following year. They had two daughters: Bunty and Vivian. One of Duncan's paintings, *Saint Bride*, shows angels with the faces of Janet and Christine carrying St Bride to the Holy Land.

Like her older sister, Dolly, Christine joined Mary's police force. Bunty recalled meeting Mary: 'I first met her in Edinburgh in the early '20s and thought she was a man. She had a monocle and was always dressed in uniform, jackboots and all.'[23]

Christine's marriage to John Duncan ended in 1926. She sent her children to Belgium to stay with her sister, Elsie, while she decided what to do next. She shut her eyes and stuck a pin in a world map; the pin landed on Cape Town. So she borrowed £50 from another sister, Dolly, collected the children and set sail for South Africa, where she worked amongst the poor, setting up the Service Dining Rooms, which provided nourishing meals for a few cents. Bunty took over the Service Dining Rooms from her mother, and it is still providing food and a meeting place today.

Christine became a Christian Scientist in Cape Town:

Then that did not satisfy her and she joined some obscure religion, which she kept very secret … She believed in reincarnation and had great affinity with the Egyptians. She said in a previous incarnation that she had been one of the daughters of Aknaten. I am glad that when she came back the last time that her head had gone into shape again. You may remember that those little daughters had very peculiar egg shaped heads.[24]

Christine often came back to England, and became the first warden at the Chalice Well at Glastonbury in 1959. By this time she was a widow; her second husband, Colonel Sandeman, had died. In 1964, while visiting Chalice Well, she was called away to look after her sister, Mary, who she cared for until Mary died in the same year. Bunty said of her mother: 'She was quite a girl … My two daughters loved her very much and she loved them.'[25] Mary left the whole of her estate to Christine, who died in 1972.

In a photograph of some of the Allen family, taken when they were living in Bristol, Mary's parents appear somewhat stern and forbidding. Margaret, her mother, is grey haired and rather worn looking; Thomas is still a fine figure, whom the years had treated more kindly. Of the four of their children in the photograph, Christine looks up almost fearfully at the photographer, while Janet, who is wearing a large cross, is gazing away from the camera with an abstracted look. Both are as attractive as their description in Gerry Fenge's book suggests. The young man in the photograph is identified as Arthur Denys, the inventor, who has a humorous expression.

Evidently taken before Mary left home, the photograph has much to tell us. Although clearly posed by the photographer, it still suggests a bond between Mary and Janet, who has her arm draped across Mary's shoulders, and Mary and Denys, whose elbow is on Mary's knee. Mary herself shows no sign of the masculine appearance she adopted soon after leaving home: she is fashionably dressed, in a high-necked ruffled blouse, her hair arranged in an elaborate style. Her father is standing beside her, but with his back turned to her; her mother has an expression of long-suffering. Mary, square-jawed and rather plain, stares boldly at the camera. Her stubborn restless nature is evident from her taut posture and firm mouth.

Mary is not found anywhere on the 1901 census, when the Allen family were living at 39 Mount Avenue, Picton House, Ealing. She is heard of next in February 1909, by which time she is an active militant suffragette. In a court appearance, she gives her father's address, 29 The Mount, Winterbourne, Bristol, although it is unlikely that she is actually living there.

In a studio portrait of Mary taken shortly after the family group, she looks younger than her 30 years: tall and slim in a tight-fitting overcoat, wearing a fashionable hat with a veil, a hunger strike medal pinned to her lapel. She carries a large satchel, stencilled with the words 'VOTES FOR WOMEN 1d'. This is where Mary's independent life begins.

2

THIS SUFFRAGETTE NONSENSE

'As a girl I had lived in the west of England, in a home that was an ideal of security and peace. As was considered correct in my time and class, I had always dismissed with a delicate shudder the whole subject of Women's Suffrage.'[1]

Mary Allen's account of her leaving home to become a suffragette, written some thirty years after the event, is worth quoting at length, as it underlines some of her defining characteristics, including an obsession with her health, and her stubborn determination:

If I felt any criticism of home conditions, it was perhaps that [the] parental régime was somewhat strict, though it was lightened in my case because I was often ill, and it seemed that I might grow up to be a permanent semi-invalid. No one thought at that time that I would later accept a task needing so much activity and concentration that only an exceptional physique could enable me to carry it out.

Having had my interest aroused in the Suffrage question, I went home, entered my father's study, and asked him to explain the whole subject to me. Second thoughts are not always best; had I waited, perhaps I should never have dared to face him with such a request! And then perhaps I should not have been writing this book now. He drew down his brows, and looked more stern than I had ever seen him.

'I cannot discuss such folly!' he answered. 'As for you, I wish you to think no more about it.'

But I was my father's daughter. I gathered my courage together and said I would never give it up. There was a sinister silence for a moment.

'Either you give up this Suffragette nonsense absolutely and for good – or you leave this house!'

In those Edwardian days, such an ultimatum, to a girl, was inconceivably dreadful. I was trained for no occupation. Where could I go? What could I do? But above the terror in my heart rose a strong determination not to be forced into an injustice. As steadily as I could, I agreed to leave home …

He was, I knew, unflinching in his decision. Yet he was extraordinarily generous. He continued and even increased my allowance, despite our disagreement. This meant that I was not forced to earn my living as a Suffragette, but could work in an honorary capacity for the movement. This meant a great deal to me.

Thomas Allen was a stern father, but Mary loved and respected him. Indeed, he was the model for the many strong men who influenced Mary's beliefs and actions. She shared her father's conservative Victorian values, even when she herself was breaking away from them. It is one of the paradoxes of Mary's make-up that what she saw as good for the generality of women did not apply to her. She was a special case.

❧❧❧

Mary's motives in joining the women's suffrage movement were complex. She was undoubtedly inspired by the cause and sincere in her commitment. But there was another dimension. Throughout her life Mary was eager for new and exciting outlets for her considerable energies. Now, as a spinster in her early thirties, she wanted to make her mark. Her elder brother, Thomas, was married and living in Argentina with his wife and two sons; and her sisters, Dolly and Elsie, and two more brothers, Denys and Herbert, were also married. Mary was an ageing cuckoo in the nest and a rebellious role-model for Janet and Christine, her impressionable younger sisters.

In her second volume of autobiography, *A Woman at the Cross Roads*, she describes this restless energy: 'From my early girlhood I have been a mental rebel – questioning conditions long taken for granted – eager for action of some kind, and ready to fling myself into any enterprise, however unprecedented, that promised results.' (p.56) Only in retrospect (*A Woman at the Cross Roads* was written in 1934), was she aware that her need for activity was of more importance to her than the actual cause into which she poured her energies. She certainly never regretted being a suffragette. She found a new home for her enthusiasm for novelty and industry among vibrant women, many of whom became lifelong friends. But she did later modify her views on how the vote might best have been gained for women.

There is no record of what Mary was doing in the decade between her leaving school, and joining Mrs Pankhurst's Women's Social and Political

Union (WSPU). It is impossible to imagine that she sat in a parlour waiting to be married – she was far too spirited a person to do next to nothing. But she was, as she says in *Lady in Blue*, 'trained for no occupation' (p.14), and she may well have been aware already that marriage was not an option for her. We know that she and her sisters travelled a great deal and had a degree of freedom. It wasn't a dull life.

Mary never returned to her father's house during his lifetime. This was not such a dramatic fate as it sounds: Thomas Allen only lived a few more years, and after his death, the family home was once again open to her. Her decision to turn her back on home and family might have been different had her father not agreed to support her financially. Mary was accustomed to the comfortable life of an Edwardian gentlewoman.

Exactly when Mary's confrontation with her father over the question of women's suffrage took place is unclear: all we can say with certainty is that she was still living at the family home in Bristol at the end of 1907, when she appears on a family photograph taken on the occasion of the wedding of her brother, Herbert, on 31 December. Mary, slim and elegant, has a baby on her lap, and she is smiling into the camera like a contented aunt. There is no sign of the discord to come, nor of the dramatic changes she was to make in her dress and appearance.

Mary's account of her time as a suffragette* takes up a dozen pages in the first chapter of *Lady in Blue*, the last of her three autobiographical works. It is necessarily brief – *Lady in Blue* was intended as a history of her career as a police woman – and, like *A Woman at the Cross Roads*, it was written with hindsight from a distance of many years. Nonetheless, it is a vivid and revealing story, told with her customary enthusiasm.

Mary left her father's house to become a suffragette, 'inspired by a speech I heard, given by Miss Annie Kenney, on the subject of Women's Suffrage'. (p.15) We do not know when Mary heard Annie Kenney speak, but it was probably in 1907, the year in which Annie Kenney was appointed WSPU organiser for the West of England, based in Bristol. The first of a series of grand meetings was held in the Victoria Rooms, Clifton, Bristol, on 8 November 1907. By the beginning of 1909, Mary was fully involved in the organisation of activities in the West of England, and making newspaper headlines as an active suffragette.

---

* The word 'suffragette' was coined in 1906 by a *Daily Mail* reporter, Charles Hands, to distinguish militant campaigners from those suffragists who hoped to gain the vote through peaceful constitutional means. The two words later became interchangeable.

Annie Kenney, Mary's inspiration, grew up in rural West Yorkshire, where she joined the local branch of the Independent Labour Party (ILP). After hearing Christabel Pankhurst address an ILP meeting, she joined the WSPU in 1905. Annie was utterly devoted to the cause of women's suffrage: Emmeline Pethick-Lawrence, a driving force in the WSPU, who worked closely with Annie, declared that, 'her strength lay in complete surrender of mind, soul and body to a single idea'.[2] Annie and Christabel became close friends, and went to political meetings together to shout at speakers, calling on them to support the cause of Women's Suffrage. They instigated protests at public meetings, and became the first suffragettes to be arrested and charged with assault when they interrupted a Liberal Party election meeting on 13 October 1905 in the Free Trade Hall in Manchester and, having refused either to stop shouting ('Will the Liberal government give women the vote?') or to leave, allegedly kicked and spat at a police officer. The two women refused to pay fines of 5s each, and were sent to Strangeways Prison – Annie for three days, Christabel for five. They had deliberately behaved in a manner which would lead to arrest, and they had no intention of paying fines: prison was their goal. Emmeline Pankhurst, Christabel's mother, offered to pay the fines, but Annie and Christabel refused to allow her to do so. On their release from prison, they were greeted by large crowds of supporters: suffragette prisoner releases were always celebrated with flowers, speeches and banquets – events which were sufficiently dramatic to be reported in the newspapers, giving the WSPU welcome publicity and showing their solidarity in a positive and celebratory light.

Annie Kenney went to prison many times, and went on frequent hunger strikes and endured force-feeding. She was a woman of striking appearance, described thus by Sylvia Pankhurst:

> She was eager and impulsive in manner, with a thin, haggard face, and restless knotted hands, from one of which a finger had been torn by the machinery it was her work to attend. Her abundant, loosely dressed golden hair was the most youthful looking thing about her … The wild, distraught expression, apt to occasion solicitude, was found on better acquaintance to be less common than a bubbling merriment, in which the crow's feet wrinkled quaintly about a pair of twinkling, bright blue eyes.[3]

Annie's background was utterly different from Mary's: although both came from large families (Annie was one of eleven children, Mary one of ten), Annie's family were poor textile workers, and she started work in the mill at the age of 10. Mary saw her as a preacher with, 'like Peter the Hermit, exceptional powers'.[4] (Peter the Hermit was a twelfth-century monk who rallied an army of 20,000 peasants to fight in the First Crusade.) Mary was well aware of the social and ideological gulf between herself and Annie Kenney. Her 'conversion' is, therefore, a remarkable testament to Annie Kenney's charisma.

❧ ☙

Mary 'went to Mrs Pankhurst, and asked her to use me in whatever capacity she thought best'.[5] Emmeline Pankhurst came from an upper-middle-class family but, unlike Mary's, her parents were political radicals, who encouraged free thinking in their children. She became involved with the Women's Franchise League, a pressure group set up in 1889 with the aim of gaining the vote for all women, not just for single women. The Women's Franchise League proved to be short-lived and ill-supported, and she joined the newly formed Independent Labour Party in 1894, but by 1903 Emmeline lost patience with the inactivity of the ILP, many of whose members were antagonistic to the whole notion of women's suffrage, and founded the Women's Social and Political Union (WSPU), a breakaway group from the National Union of Women's Suffrage Societies (NUWSS).

Mrs Pankhurst rallied her troops with the words: 'Women, we must do the work ourselves. We must have an independent women's movement. Come to my house tomorrow and we will arrange it!'[6] Their motto, 'Deeds, not Words', predicted the militant course the WSPU was to take: unlike the NUWSS, which was committed to peaceful constitutional activities, and remained so throughout the period of the struggle for the vote.

Mary is fulsome in her praise of Emmeline Pankhurst in *Lady in Blue*: 'her quiet voice, her magnetic eyes and her deep sincerity were releasing forces in the world whose power has not even yet been calculated … Some day … Mrs Pankhurst will be recognised as one of the greatest figures of the twentieth century.' (p.15)

❧ ☙

Throughout her life, Mary was susceptible to the charms of charismatic women, to whom she gave heartfelt devotion. Moreover, Emmeline Pankhurst was a woman from a background similar to her own: a leader Mary felt able to follow without question.

Campaigns for women's suffrage had started in the late 1860s, but militant tactics were not generally employed before 1906. The WSPU's original intention was to recruit women from every class to the cause, but according to one of her biographers Emmeline Pankhurst 'proceeded to lead the militant suffragette movement away from its original working-class constituency and to establish it within the upper-class drawing rooms of Kensington and Chelsea'.[7] Although Mary Allen had been attracted to suffrage by the working-class Annie Kenney, the WSPU was, by the time she joined its ranks, led mainly by women of her own kind.

The public perception of the movement as a middle and upper-class entity allowed male newspapers writers, reporting on a meeting convened by the Women's Liberal Federation, to condemn those suffragettes present for unbecoming behaviour:

> It is doubtful whether a more dramatic political meeting has ever been held in London. Women summoned it, women turned it into a Bedlam; and five-sixths of the audience consisted of women. Yet men had to do the dirty work of putting the women out. At times the scenes were as violent and distasteful as if the Royal Albert Hall had been turned into a low public-house, on a wild Saturday night in the slums. Shrieking women carried out shoulder-high; men trying to gag them with their hands; all sense of decency lost for the moment – it was a melancholy and disheartening spectacle; and the pity of it was that there were, very often, women who in saner moments would be treated with tender respect as gentle ladies.[8]

The author of these remarks concurs with Lloyd George who, in his speech at this meeting, warned that the forthcoming electoral reform Bill 'could only be lost through the folly, the lunacy of some of those who thought that they were helping the cause of Woman's Suffrage'. Some commentators even went so far as to compare suffragette disruption of political meetings with attacks of epilepsy.[9] It was not unusual in Edwardian England for men to label forceful women who held radical ideas as simply mad.

Mary was inclined to share this male view of the rank and file activists outside the inner circle to which she aspired. She despised undisciplined women. They were, she said in *A Woman at the Cross Roads*:

> Simply swayed by a burning emotional enthusiasm, in which intelligence played a minor part. A few of the most violent among them were guilty of every variety of hysterical exaggeration; they developed a kind of sex-mania, a hostility towards men that made them almost snort with rage at any suggestion that co-operation with them was an essential – even an unavoidable part of our programme. (p.62)

It is certainly true that Mary herself never showed 'hostility towards men'. She did not dislike men; indeed, she frequently expressed admiration for strong male leaders, whose sartorial and oratorical style she emulated and whose opinions influenced her own.

Mary worked hard for the WSPU in the south-west of England, organising meetings, selling copies of *Votes for Women* on the streets, speaking to large audiences of women, writing articles for suffragette papers, and publicising Self-Denial Week, at which she was photographed with her colleagues beside a barrel-organ, her face almost completely obscured by an enormous hat.

Inevitably, Mary moved to London, the hub of suffragette activities, to work more closely with Emmeline Pankhurst and take part in militant activities. She had discovered a flair for organisation which was recognised by her colleagues, who appointed her chief marshall at the lavish funeral parade in London for Emily Wilding Davison, who died after being trampled by the king's horse at the Epsom Derby in 1913. She never became a prime mover in the suffragette hierarchy, but by throwing herself into the WSPU with enthusiasm and vigour, she gained valuable experience for the future in recruiting and training women.

3

SUFFERING IN THE CAUSE OF WOMANKIND

Inspired by Emmeline Pankhurst, Mary was prepared to take part in breaches of the peace. 'When I first went to her, I had sacrificed much. She asked me to sacrifice more.'[1] Mary volunteered to take part in an attempt on 24 February 1909 to present a petition to Parliament:

On a certain morning, forty of us, in our long skirts and big hats, tried to force our way through a cordon of stalwart policemen and enter the House of Commons. Of course we were arrested. Men from the idle crowd that stood about the entrance roared with laughter, yelled ribald and obscene remarks, clawed and pawed at us; and in the end the police arrested us and took us off as much for our own safety as because we had broken any law. Most of us were delicately bred women, and our horror of such a scene may be imagined; yet we were sustained by pride because we knew we were suffering in the cause of womankind.[2]

Mary was arrested for the first time. She was in her element: joined with other women like herself in a common cause. The assertion that 'most of us were delicately bred women' shows that the WSPU was already far removed from its original classless composition, at least in Mary's own experience.

The following day, *The Times* reported on these events under the headline 'Disturbance at Westminster', beginning with a vivid account of the Women's Parliament held at Caxton Hall, which preceded the deputation to Parliament:

The hall was crowded with women, and great enthusiasm prevailed. Flags and banners bearing mottoes were displayed. Mrs Pankhurst, the founder of the union, presided, and she was supported on the platform by 30 women who had promised to form the deputation and who were wearing sashes

28

of the colours of the union, on which were printed the words 'Votes for Women'. At the commencement of the proceedings the women, led by a brass band, joined in the singing of 'The Women's Marseillaise'.

This was the sort of positive reporting that the WSPU leadership wanted. They were protesting at the absence in the king's speech of a measure giving votes to women, and intended to take their demand for such a policy change to Mr Asquith, the prime minister. The deputation, led by Emmeline Pethick-Lawrence, had attempted to rush at a body of police constables barring their way into the strangers' entrance to the Houses of Parliament. Mary was among those arrested by police officers who 'endured very patiently not merely the pushing and scratching of the "militants", but a vigorous if totally ineffective and unimpressive lashing with the tongue of sarcasm and abuse'. The protesters were taken to Cannon Row police station, charged with obstructing the police, and released when the House rose, having been bailed by Emmeline Pethick-Lawrence. Mary appears in the list of those arrested as 'Mary Alen [*sic*], 29, The Mount, Winterbury [*sic*], Bristol'. In fact, Mary was approaching her thirty-first birthday and, if we are to believe that she had been banished by her father, the address she gave to the police was false.

At Bow Street Police Court on 26 February, the magistrate said, 'it was greatly to be regretted that educated ladies should disgrace themselves in this way'. Mary was among those who, having refused to be bound over, were sentenced to one month's imprisonment and taken to Holloway Gaol.

In the report of these events in the 26 February 1909 edition of *Votes for Women*, there was a short account of Mary's reasons for joining the fray: 'Miss Mary Allen (Bristol) has had a happy home life, and now wishes to devote herself to work for women in less happy circumstances than herself.' This statement confirms the impression of a contented childhood given in *A Woman at the Cross Roads*. Interestingly, it suggests that leaving home was Mary's own choice, rather than one imposed on her by her father. This, coupled with her giving her father's address in court, suggests the possibility that her exile was not as total as Mary implied, or that it came into effect after her first arrest, rather than before.

Writing in *Lady in Blue* about her first sentence, Mary describes in some detail the conditions in women's prisons. They were, she says, 'an ordeal for ordinary people. There were no tooth-brushes, no hair-brushes, no mirrors.

Our beds were planks, our pillows coarse straw. Lights were put out at eight o'clock, and we had to be up again at 5 a.m. – very often after a sleepless night.' (p.17) One wonders who the extraordinary people were for whom prison was *not* an ordeal: perhaps those for whom hairbrushes were not a priority. Mary is still very much the genteel Edwardian lady.

Camaraderie helped the suffragettes to endure, and indeed to face further spells of imprisonment in the future. 'We tried in every way we could to keep each other's spirits up in that grey, grim place. We were determined that no one should ever be able to say – "Those Suffragettes won't dare to face a second dose." In fact, we were proud of being gaol-birds!' (p.17)

Mary's overriding concern from a personal point of view was the food:

> In the main, our food consisted of dry brown bread of dark, rough quality. We were allowed no butter, and no sweetstuffs such as jam. Indeed, we were given no sugar in any form, and our health suffered a good deal as a direct result, since a proportion of sugar is necessary to fitness. Unsweetened tea without milk was a luxury; our principal drink was just water. Skilly soups with lumps of what we believed to be horse-flesh for dinner; dry bread again for tea; no supper. (p.17)

She was always anxious about her own health, having been, by her own account, a delicate child: 'I was often ill, and it seemed that I might grow up to be a permanent semi-invalid.' (p.14) It is hard to reconcile this perceived frailty with Mary's later career and the fact that she lived to the age of 86. Nevertheless, sickness was a prevailing preoccupation with Mary while she was in prison, and her pleas for special treatment met with mixed success:

> From the first, I was more fortunate than some, for I was allowed milk in consideration of my health. The others had no milk … Once or twice during our confinement I fell ill and asked to see Dr. Mary Gordon, our prison inspector, meaning to plead with her for a more healthy diet. But my request was always refused. (p.17)

Communication between suffragette prisoners was the biggest problem, and the greatest trial, for they were forbidden to speak, or to use pencils and paper:

> We were forbidden, under pain of severe punishment, to communicate with each other. But our wits soon overcame the ban. We had to stitch

men's shirts as our principal employment in the prison. So we used to collect scraps of waste material, secrete them, and stitch messages on them.

These messages not only circulated freely throughout the prison itself, usually inside cotton reels and under the unsuspecting eyes of our wardresses, but used to get smuggled outside whenever we had information that we wished to communicate to Mrs. Pankhurst at Headquarters. We were, of course, allowed no pencils or paper.

Our busy needles were not confined to this single outlet for our joie-de-vivre, after our allotted pile of shirts was done. We gave the prison authorities even better value than they bargained for on the shirts themselves, just to show what model prisoners we were.

We embroidered 'VOTES FOR WOMEN' round the tail of each shirt we handled. Personally I put this indelible legend on over a hundred shirts. They were made of unbleached calico, and would probably have lasted for many years; sometimes I wonder if any of them are still being worn at Wormwood Scrubs and Pentonville – the 'regimental banners' of a forgotten cause! (p.18)

Overall, Mary is surprisingly sanguine about her imprisonment. She declares that she and her fellow suffragette inmates 'worked hard and cheerfully, and we were well treated in many ways. It was noticeable in those years that the police and the prison officials were altogether kinder and more lenient than the general public were to us.' (p.19) But she found the silence – even the prison officers were not allowed to speak to them – appalling.

A dinner for released prisoners was given at the Inns of Courts on 24 March 1909. In the report in *Votes for Women* of 2 April 1909, Mary is quoted as praising the solidarity of her fellow-prisoners:

Miss Mary Allen of Bristol said that she had admired women before she joined the WSPU, but, having been to Holloway, she felt that no one knew their capacity for combining and standing up for one another. She had been unfairly punished for some breach of discipline, and all the women had appealed to the governor on her behalf, and had succeeded in getting her two days' solitary confinement reduced to one.

Mary liked to portray herself as a popular figure, and perhaps she was. But a prison governor, acceding to an appeal for clemency from a group of prisoners, stretches the imagination.

Shortly after Mary's release from prison, work began in earnest to expand WSPU operations in the west of England. There were already five branches by May 1909, and in *Votes for Women* on 14 May it is reported that:

> We are concentrating just now on Cardiff, where we have started active work. Miss Mary Allen, Miss Blathwayt, and I [Annie Kenney], with the help of Miss Jackson ... have taken the Paget Rooms in Penarth, and are arranging a meeting for Thursday May 20th at 3 pm for women only.

Other meetings in Cardiff followed, in June, Mary was acting as voluntary organiser in Annie Kenney's absence, and on 25 June she is reported as addressing a meeting in Cardiff. Mary has risen rapidly through the ranks, and attained a trusted position. She is introduced more fully to the WSPU membership in the 2 July 1909 *Votes for Women*:

> Miss Mary Allen, of Bristol, who has been working with Miss Annie Kenney in Cardiff and Newport has sacrificed her home ties to work for this movement, feeling that those who have money and leisure ought to play the part that is impossible to women dependent on their earnings. She has already served one month's imprisonment.

It is clear from this that Mary's allowance was more than adequate for her needs.

Responsibilities of office never deterred the most militant WSPU members from activities that might lead to their imprisonment, leaving others to take over their more routine work. Mary left her post to go on a window-breaking foray, and she was arrested again on 14 July 1909. In court, two days later, she said, 'I did it intentionally, and when I saw the women arrested I did it as a protest against Mr Asquith in refusing our members.' The prime minister's obduracy, while not excusing criminal acts, certainly explained them: unable to get a hearing, the suffragettes felt they had no choice but to draw attention to their cause through acts of violence.

However strong the commitment to the cause, participating in lawbreaking required a good deal of courage, and Mary describes vividly her feelings when she was 'given the duty' of breaking the windows of the Home Office:

I accepted the commission, but it called for almost more courage than I possessed. It was one thing to cause a minor riot with two score of supporters at one's back, and quite another to act thus alone. Three times I rode round London on a horse-bus before I could force my feet to descend, in passing Downing Street, and carry me to my objective.[3]

This was not window-smashing on a large scale: we learn from *A Woman at the Cross Roads* that Mary 'earned the second sentence by breaking a glass panel in the Home Office door' – an illegal act, but small when compared to the campaigns to come, where large numbers of shops and offices in high streets were attacked. We should not underestimate Mary's spirit and determination, however: 'No-one at that day seemed to realise what any agony of mind it cost us to drive ourselves to tasks so entirely repugnant.' (pp.58–9)

After her arrest on 14 July 1909, Mary received her second prison sentence, one month's imprisonment in the second division. This was just after the first suffragette hunger strike, carried out by Marion Dunlop, as a protest at not being treated as a political prisoner and sentenced to the first division, where prisoners were allowed visitors, writing materials and their own food and clothing. Mary gives her own account of the WSPU's decision to use hunger strikes as a weapon:

> It had been resolved at headquarters that unless we were treated as 'political prisoners' we would protest as strongly as it was in our power. From this resolution came the last resource of despair – the hunger strike. It must be confessed that this programme was carried out against the wishes of Mrs Pankhurst, who considered it dangerous, not only to our health but as a precedent, though she fully conceded that it might be effective.[4]

In fact, Mrs Pankhurst went on to endure numerous hunger strikes herself, severely compromising her own health.

The conditions in which Mary was held when on hunger strike were to be starker than those she had experienced during her first term of imprisonment. She recalled in *Lady in Blue* that, 'All the time I was starving, I was kept solitary in a special cell reserved for troublesome prisoners – a dark, underground room with double doors, rusty locks, and stone walls, floor and ceiling. It was windowless, and was furnished simply with a wooden bed and a wooden pillow.' (p.21)

Mary had her clothes removed by force, and she was 'provided with prison dress, marked with big black arrows'. (p.20) Reasoning that the prison authorities would release her rather than allow her to starve to death, she decided to become a hunger striker. Writing some twenty-five years after these events, her description of the way in which the authorities tried to break her strike is vivid:

> when I had neither eaten nor drunk for two days, they brought in a kettle of boiling water, a teapot, some creamy milk and some lump sugar. They made the tea; they held the steaming teapot under my nose. It almost drove me mad. My tongue was like leather with thirst, and the hot, fragrant smell started the saliva running at the back of my throat. I just shook my head and shut my eyes.
>
> After two more days they brought mincemeat and chicken into my cell. Slices of white chicken's breast in savoury brown gravy were offered to me. They clattered teacups, poured milk with a bubbling sound, and tinkled bits of ice in a bowl.
>
> I shut out the thought of the delicious dainties – the healing ice for my burning throat, the rich gravy which could end my terrible exhaustion. (pp.21–22)

Mary was released after five days, in which she claimed to have had neither food nor water. She was the first to receive the WSPU's hunger strike medal, presented by Emmeline Pethick-Lawrence at St James's Hall in August 1909. The medal was engraved with the words 'for valour', and attached to a ribbon in the movement's colours of purple, white and green. The ceremony is described in *Votes for Women*:

> The Hunger strikers at St James's Hall
>
> Mrs Pethick Lawrence ... announced that a commemorative medal had been struck, and would be presented to each of the hunger strikers in recognition of what they had suffered for the cause.
>
> Miss Mary Allen was the first of the recipients, and, as she stepped to the front of the platform amid deafening cheers, Mrs Pankhurst pinned one of the medals on her breast, at the same time remarking: 'Dear woman soldier in the women's army, I thank you for having destroyed once and for ever the terrors of prison, and for having shown the greatest, the strongest, and the richest Government that the world has ever seen that a Government cannot safely ignore justice, and that if they do, the spirit of weak women will prove the stronger.' (Loud applause.)
>
> It is a trite axiom that those who are most worthy of applause are always the most modest, and this spirit of self-negation was strikingly apparent in

the speeches of the 'hunger strikers', each of whom gave a short account of her prison experiences.

Miss Mary Allen said that she was grateful from her heart to Miss Wallace Dunlop for having shown the way. In her punishment cell she fainted – probably through want of food – and when she awoke, cold and weary, she sang the 'Woman's Marseillaise' to cheer herself, and to her delight heard a 'Bravo!' from the next cell, whose occupant joined in, and they both sang it through again together. On the sixth day she was taken to hospital, where the casuistic argument was brought forward that she might safely break her resolution, as in that place first, second, and third divisions were all one!

This is perhaps the last time anyone describes Mary's demeanour as 'modest'. It is completely at odds with her later reputation for arrogance and self-advertisement. But people change, and it is entirely believable that she still retained the restrained manners of a middle-class young lady, instilled in her by her parents and governesses.

Mary seems to have been a well-known person among the militant suffragette community: Gladys Roberts of Leeds, formerly a solicitor's clerk, kept a secret shorthand diary while she was in Holloway, and her entry for Saturday, 17 July 1909 reads:

> Tremendous excitement – Mary Allen has just come down to the cell next to mine. She broke more windows when she heard Herbert Gladstone's reply [to petitions for political prisoner status – he saw no reason why he should take action]. It has quite bucked me up.[5]

Mary Blathwayt, a diarist and suffragette who lived at Batheaston in Somerset, records the reception for Mary when she returned to Bristol after this second prison term:

> 4 Sep. [1909] We drove down to Bristol station, and formed up into a procession; it was to receive Mrs Dove Willcox and Miss Mary Allen, two ex prisoners and hunger strikers on their return to Bristol. A military band had promised to play, but they declined at the last moment. First came a carriage containing Mrs Dove Willcox, and Miss Mary Allen; Annie Kenney and some others walked just behind it and then followed a long procession of ladies with banners and tricolour. I helped to carry a banner marked Finland. A very long line of carriages followed. The roads were muddy and it rained a little at first.[6]

The reference to Finland is explained in *Votes for Women*, 10 September 1909:

> A rousing welcome home was given last Saturday by the Bristol members to their brave hunger strikers, Mrs Dove Willcox and Miss Mary Allen. A very fine procession of women and men, with nine banners and tricolour flags innumerable, followed by a long trail of carriages, marched four miles through crowds of people to Henley Grove. One happy feature was a series of flags bearing the names of countries which have already taken the step of recognising women as citizens.

The two women were each presented with a belt and clasp by the local WSPU members.

Mary's third and final arrest was a result of breaking a window at the Inland Revenue offices in Bristol, on 13 November 1909. She had heard:

> that Mr Churchill, who had refused to receive a deputation of the good and quiet Suffragettes, was to receive a deputation of pilots, and she sent a 'Message' through the windows of the Inland Revenue office. The message ran: 'A protest against a Government which receives deputations from men and refuses to hear the grievances of women.'

For this offence, Mary was sentenced to one month's imprisonment without hard labour:

Window-breakers sentenced

> Three suffragettes, Nurse Pitman, Vera Wentworth, and Mary Allen, appeared at Bristol Police Court on Saturday, charged with damaging public buildings. Pitman, who broke the plate-glass windows at the post-office, damage £15 was committed for trial. Wentworth, for breaking the windows at the Liberal Club, was ordered to pay the damage and a fine of 20s. Refusing to pay, she was sentenced to 14 days' imprisonment. She demanded to be treated as a political offender. The Bench ordered her detention in the Second Division. Allen, on whom the same penalty was passed, stated that she would continue to protest against the Government by smashing windows. While in the cells the prisoners sang suffragette songs.[7]

Vera Wentworth went to prison a number of times, and worked as a WSPU organiser in the west of England. She was something of a loose cannon, carrying out unauthorised acts of violence and intimidation, singling out Asquith for her unwanted attentions, harassing him at Lympne church and on holiday at Clovelly.

Mary Blathwayt wrote in her diary on 13 November: 'This morning we went down to the police court. Vera Wentworth, Miss Pitman and Mary Allen were all tried. Vera W. and Mary Allen each have 14 days in the 2nd division.'[8]

This time, Mary began a hunger strike, 'the last resource of despair',[9] as soon as she arrived at the prison to serve her sentence. The authorities, by now experienced in dealing with hunger strikers, sent her immediately to the prison hospital where, after two days, they began to feed her forcibly:

> while six wardresses held me down, the prison doctors beat up an egg in one and a-half pints of milk, and forced it into my stomach, through the nose in two minutes.
>
> One and a half pints in two minutes! Of course I was violently sick, getting rid of all the nourishment which had been so brutally shovelled into me. I developed a shivering terror whenever I thought of my next forcible meal. But I would not give in.
>
> Finally they made me so very ill that I had to be released, my digestion being permanently affected.[10]

At the time, Mary described her suffering to her comrades, and it was reported in *Votes for Women* that:

> Those who are inclined to accept Mr Gladstone's perverted statements as to the mild discomfort of forcible feeding should read the accounts given by the women who have actually endured it. Miss Allen speaks of the 'terrible inflammation of the nostril' caused by the tube, and a feeling as if the whole back of the nose and throat is being dragged out with the tube. Both she and Miss Wentworth describe the use of the gag and throat tube.

The after-effects of forcible feeding have been recorded in Allen family legend: in a letter written 100 years after these events, Margaret Bateman, Mary's great-niece, recalls that 'ever after she had stomach trouble. "History" does not relate of what type.'[11]

Apart from these references to vomiting, and the effects on her digestion, Mary says nothing about the pain and indignity of forcible feeding, which were considerable.

That she suffered greatly is not in question: a fellow-prisoner, Nurse Pitman, wrote about hearing 'the cries and deep moans of Miss Mary Allen' who was in a nearby cell, and 'who was fed twice a day'.

Mary and Vera Wentworth were released on 26 November 1909 and, although the time of their release was kept secret by the authorities, 'a crowd of some two hundred people assembled outside the prison quite early, ready to welcome them'. (*Votes for Women*, 3 December 1909) However harsh the conditions she had suffered, the acclaim she received on her release was gratifying for Mary, who was learning to love being the centre of attention.

4

NURSED BACK TO HEALTH

Conditions in women's prisons were not of much interest to the general population in Edwardian England. Apart from a handful of reformers, the better-off preferred to close their eyes and ears. It was nothing to do with them. But this was to change when the hitherto respectable middle-class ladies who became suffragettes experienced prison life for themselves. Mary describes in some detail the food, the strict regime, and the cells, but without expressing any direct opinion on the justice of subjecting women – whatever their crimes – to such privations. Her attitude, as recorded in *A Woman at the Cross Roads* and *Lady in Blue*, is a mixture of factual objectivity, and excitement at finding herself in this predicament ('I think we did rather well as novices in the criminal world. But for all our pranks we worked hard and cheerfully.').[1] This is not to say that she was unmoved by the fate of women prisoners, and particularly that of her fellow suffragettes. She simply chose not to write down her emotional response. Complaining was not Mary's style.

Other suffragette prisoners were more candid. Mrs Pankhurst was characteristically forthright in an article in the *Daily Telegraph*, in which she described the absolute silence, the coarse prison clothes, the meagre dimensions of the cells, and the lack of privacy when bathing.[2] Accounts of forcible feeding are extremely harrowing, and modern commentators point out the abusive nature of this brutal practice:

For many of these women, the worst feature of prison life was the 'public' violation of their bodies when being forcibly fed … Although the word 'rape' is not used in the personal accounts of force fed victims, the instrumental invasion of the body, accompanied by overpowering physical force, great suffering and humiliation was akin to it.[3]

A warder at Holloway, Agnes Resbury, recorded her memories of prison life, and she declared of the suffragettes: 'I know they were out to do good and make it better for us women, although some of their methods were bad.' Agnes Resbury seems to have been an honest woman, and a kind one, if a little fearful of association with suffragettes. Emmeline Pethick-Lawrence invited her to attend a suffragette procession, at which:

> some of them seeing me came running up to me and said, 'Here is our darling Miss Resbury from Holloway Prison, used to give us our work,' and several came round to me.
>
> I said, 'Go away, don't come and talk to me now.'
>
> 'Oh,' they said, 'darling we're not in prison now and can talk to you.'
>
> I said, 'I've just come to see the procession and I can't stay if you get round me.'

Agnes Resbury confirms Mary's story about marking the shirts they were set to sew: 'I found worked on the tail of the vest was, in large letters, "Votes for Women".'[4]

Questions were asked in the House of Commons repeatedly about the conditions in which suffragettes were detained in Holloway Prison. On 7 November 1906, the Home Secretary, Herbert Gladstone, stated that:

> The prison life of the ladies now in Holloway differs from that of ordinary prisoners. They enjoy frequent visits from their friends, they are allowed books, newspapers, and writing materials freely; they can carry on their professional work as far as possible, and they are exempted from prison work if they so wish … [Their] cells are neither dark nor damp, and the prisoners themselves do not complain of them.[5]

These remarks refer to prisoners in the first division, where conditions were superior to those experienced by petty criminals, vagrants and prostitutes. Very few suffragettes were so classified (that is, as political prisoners), despite numerous demands from them, made in court and in communications from their cells. The Home Secretary said repeatedly that decisions over whether to commit women to the first or the second division were in the hands of magistrates, and none of his concern. 'None of those placed in the second division will be liable to more than one week's imprisonment in default of paying their fines.'[6] This was certainly not always the case: Mary herself was sentenced to a month in the second division in July 1909.

Mrs Pankhurst persuaded James Keir Hardie, the first Independent Labour Party Member of Parliament, a close friend of her daughter Sylvia, and a supporter of women's suffrage, that an inspection of conditions at Holloway was necessary, and to that end a deputation was made. Mary, who had served two sentences in Holloway, the second involving a hunger strike, was appointed by Mrs Pankhurst to represent the WSPU. Gladys Roberts wrote in her diary:

> 13th August 1909. Accompanied by Mary Allen, the two ministers [Keir Hardie and Herbert Gladstone, the Home Secretary] and some colleagues made a tour of inspection on August 13. Although no public report followed, a change was soon noticeable in the aspects of Holloway life about which the suffragettes had most complained.[7]

No reference to this visit is made in Hansard, but according to *Votes for Women* on 20 August 1909, 'Mr Keir Hardie, Mr Greenwood MP, and Mr W.P. Byles MP, were taken over the punishment cells in Holloway Gaol on Friday last. Mr Gladstone, Miss Mary Allen (one of the released prisoners) and Mrs Byles were also present.'

After Mary's hunger strike, Mrs Pankhurst was as concerned about her poor physical condition as Mary was herself:

> When I had been nursed back to health, Mrs. Pankhurst categorically forbade me to risk further imprisonment. As I was still determined to play some part in the movement, she gave me the task of organising militant activities in a district under my own control. In addition, I had to arrange to speak at meetings, see to it that Members of Parliament were harassed with our protests, and gather recruits for our Cause. The work was not easy, nor was it always safe. At more than one meeting we were set upon – usually by men in the audience – and mishandled. Our clothes were torn, we were pelted with beastly missiles, chairs or boxes were dragged from under us. The police were our protectors far more than they were ever our adversaries.[8]

Although Mary did not participate personally in the most extreme wave of suffragette violence which began in 1912, when window-breaking progressed to bombings, arson and vandalisation on a large scale, she was fully involved in organising such operations, concurring with Emmeline Pankhurst's famous declaration that, 'The argument of the broken pane of glass is the most valuable argument in modern politics'.[9]

Mary put all her energies into the work of organising WSPU activities in the west of England. At the end of 1909, she was reported in *Votes for Women* as working in Launceston, Ramsgate and Margate, where she sold the paper and trained others to do so. It is likely that she was also writing the copy for the west of England area news: there are hints of her growing tendency to self-advertisement in the 28 January 1910 issue: 'Miss Mary Allen, who is giving her whole time and life to the work, is undertaking the organisation of sales of Votes for Women. Miss Allen has sacrificed much for the cause, and workers are rallying round her.'

Mary was posted to Hastings in February 1912, where she took over the position of organiser for Eastbourne, Bexhill, Hastings and St Leonards from Dorothy Bowker. On 23 February 1912, Mary wrote in *Votes for Women*: 'Miss Allen wishes to thank all members most heartily for the welcome she has received on taking over the work so splendidly started and carried on in the district by Miss Bowker.' In 1914 she was sent to Edinburgh, where she was expected to 'plan several so-called "Suffragette outrages"'. Mary is at pains to point out that 'it was ... an absolute condition that everything must be so planned that no one — not even an animal — could be hurt by what we did.' But her list of achievements suggests a less than strict adherence to this rule:

> We burned a timber-yard at Devonport. We blew up part of the wall of Holloway Prison, where some of our number were confined. A Velasquez painting in the Tate Gallery was slashed with a meat-chopper by the intrepid Mary Richardson. We smashed porcelain in the British Museum. The Britannia Pier at Yarmouth was burned down, and about £15,000 worth of damage was done. A bomb explosion was organised in the Botanical Gardens at Glasgow. Sargent's portrait of Henry James at the Royal Academy was slashed. The painting of the Duke of Wellington in the same gallery suffered an identical fate less than a week later.

This is a shocking catalogue of destruction, which Mary calmly justifies with the assertion that 'women, being fully fifty per cent of the population, owned fifty per cent of the nation's possessions. We were destroying what was at least half our own.'[10]

Mary was posted to Edinburgh, where she succeeded the American Lucy Burns, a New Yorker who had joined the WSPU in 1909 while on holiday in London. Lucy Burns had helped with the arrangements for a pageant and procession in Edinburgh in October of the same year, and the following month she took over as organiser: a rapid rise through the ranks.

Mary was not well received when she took up her post. On 6 May 1914, Christabel Pankhurst wrote in a letter to Janie Allen, a leading Scottish suffragette who had asked why the Edinburgh members did not get on with Mary, that:

> In Edinburgh a small handful of people ... are decidedly cantankerous, and the person who is organising for the time being [Mary] is made to feel the effect of this. These people criticise Miss Mary Allen at the present time, but profess to have had a great admiration for a previous organiser, Miss Lucy Burns.[11]

There were frictions in Edinburgh before Mary arrived. Lucy Burns seems to have been 'virtually driven away from Edinburgh, so unhappy was she because of a few members'. Christabel Pankhurst goes on with the reflection:

> I doubt whether there is any person living who, as an organiser, would entirely satisfy some people! The fact is that their attitude towards organisers is a wrong and false one, and we are determined to protect organisers from unfair and unreasonable criticism.[12]

Mary's unhappiness in Edinburgh was short-lived; within a few weeks of her taking up her post there, war was declared. Eunice Murray, an organiser for the Women's Freedom League in Scotland, recorded with a touch of *Schadenfreude* that the WSPU had 'dissolved and left all organisers unpaid; several applied to me for help to get them to their various homes'.[13]

One of the life-changing outcomes of working in the suffragette movement, for Mary and for many women, was the formation of enduring friendships. Another was their first true liberation from the patriarchal families in which they had grown up. Going home and resuming their former roles was not an option. They were changed women. 'The feeling of sisterhood that united all women was the backbone of the strength of the movement.'[14]

Some of the women Mary associated with in the WSPU went on, like her, to join Oswald Mosley's British Union of Fascists in the 1930s. These included Mary Richardson and Norah Elam (Mrs Dacre-Fox). Others have, like Mary herself, been identified as lesbians. However, as June Purvis notes, 'the difficulties of researching "lesbian" life (however defined) in the WSPU are enormous since few lesbians, in a climate hostile to their sexual orientation, left records of their lives where their lesbianism is made explicit'.[15]

Emily Hamer, in her study of twentieth-century lesbians maintains that, 'The relationship between the suffrage movement and lesbians is complex. The gaining of the vote would give women a symbolic equality with men, an equality which presumably was more important to lesbians than to women who were happy to be a man's wife.'[16] Whether or not we agree with this premise, it is certainly true that lesbian women were under the same social and economic pressure to marry as all women in Edwardian England, and the need to escape from this tyranny would have been strongest for those who felt unable to contemplate marriage. So inevitably they would be particularly strongly attracted to a movement which fought for independence from men.

Mary undoubtedly formed lasting friendships with a number of suffragettes who were lesbians, including Isobel Goldingham, who became a loyal colleague in Mary's post-war police service.

Lesbian women did not declare their sexuality as they do today. Indeed, homosexuality was regarded by many as an exclusively male phenomenon, and as Martin Pugh points out, 'this enabled women to live together without attracting much comment or suspicion – making it comparatively easy for those who did desire a lesbian relationship'.[17] It would not be possible to distinguish between the comradeship felt by women experiencing for the first time the liberating atmosphere of a wholly female environment, and a positive sexual attraction to another woman. But there are clues: in dress, occupation and comportment.

Mary's appearance and manner of dress changed dramatically after she became a pioneering policewoman. As long as she was a suffragette, she kept the surface demeanour of an Edwardian gentlewoman. She recounts in some detail her efforts to maintain, during her periods of imprisonment, the elaborate hairstyle which we see in Allen family photographs:

> I had very long hair in those days. Any woman will realise what that meant to me, in prison with no brush or mirror!
>
> Our duties included cleaning our own cells. I soon realised that if I polished up my dustpan till it shone, and stood it on the stool in my cell, I could kneel down before it and get reflection enough to enable me to plait my hair, and set my ugly prison cap at its least unbecoming angle.
>
> At our first attendance at prison chapel, my neighbours risked increased severities by whispering to me to ask how I had managed to turn out so tidily.[18]

Mary was described later by a fellow-prisoner, Grace Roe, as 'very feminine, very delicate'.[19] She still had her long hair and fashionable clothes as late as 1912, when she was photographed in Hastings, sharing a WSPU platform with Mrs Pankhurst.[20] The transformation in her appearance coincides with her donning a police uniform which, once her hair was cropped, was joined by a monocle and leather boots.

❧❧❧

There is an almost religious intensity to Mary's commitment to the WSPU. She describes in *Lady in Blue* her initial attraction to the movement as a conversion; Mrs Pankhurst as 'my leader'; her participation as a 'sacrifice'; and her own identity as 'one of the chosen'. (pp.13–16) Although this is not the place to investigate the origins of religious experience, it is perhaps worth noting that three of Mary's sisters were deeply religious, one of them becoming a Benedictine nun. Mary was committed to the other women in the WSPU with an intensity which she showed in her relationships with women throughout her life (perhaps not surprising given her closeness to her four sisters). She relished the values of the WSPU, with its strict hierarchy and its own uniform and medals, and she joined in violent activities with alacrity. Mary was always to be particularly attracted to uniforms, and she readily adopted the official colours of the movement (purple, white and green), and its ribbons and medals, which she treasured.

Why Mary became a suffragette is not entirely clear: she had no personal experience of the extremes of poverty and social injustice suffered by working-class women, which Annie Kenney described so forcefully in her inspiring speeches; indeed, Mary had never been obliged to work for her living at all. Her motives seem to have been complex: first, she wanted a change of lifestyle. We cannot know whether or not she identified herself as a lesbian before she left home; but no doubt opportunities for marriage – the only realistic escape from the paternal home for middle-class women – had presented themselves and been found uncongenial. Secondly, Mary wanted a vote for herself, as a single educated woman. She may well have wanted it for all women when she heard Annie Kenney speak and was converted; but as the WSPU became more and more the home of well-to-do conservative ladies, the fight became her focus, rather than the true justification for that fight. Working women were as far from her own sphere of experience as the elephants at the zoo: she was aware of their existence, but their daily lives were of little interest, and almost beyond imagining. Thirdly, Mary was a moral crusader. We shall see that her attitude to policing women was patronising and prudish, viewing women as in need of protection from their own folly and weakness. To Mary, women's suffrage was about gaining the vote for the 'right' women: that is, single women over thirty, like herself, who would be able to advise and direct lesser women in how to live decent lives.

Militant suffragette activity came to an end with the outbreak of war in 1914:

> I was actively – and shall I admit it, delightedly – planning some further burnings of empty houses, in which we had been successful of late, and preparing sundry other activities which should inconvenience the Government to the maximum possible extent, when the news came to Edinburgh that England was involved in war.
>
> The thing was like a thunderclap; and on its heels came a reverberation that startled and surprised us even more. For Mrs. Pankhurst sent unmistakable orders that we Suffragettes were instantly to 'Cease Fire!'
>
> We were to drop our private struggle with those in power, and offer ourselves as the first volunteers to help the Government in its dark hour.
>
> I won't pretend that we liked it! We were heart and soul in our fight to gain recognition for women.[21]

Mary was always loyal to the Empire, as were most middle- and upper-class women in Edwardian England. She was eager to devote herself to the war effort but, like her fellow suffragettes, she found it difficult to locate a niche in which she could serve:

> The sudden disbanding of our Suffragette groups was for many of us a bewildering blow. We had worked for Suffrage for so long that we did not know where else to turn when seeking to service our country. Many became nurses, some joined canteens and factories. I was offered a job in a Needlework Guild, which infuriated me because I wanted action.[22]

The Representation of the People Act (1918) gave the vote to eight and a half million women over 30 years old who were householders, householders' wives, graduates, or occupiers of property with an annual rent of £5 or more. Ten years later, women were granted the vote at the age of 21, on equal terms with men.

A large number of suffragette women went on to join the first Women Police Service, and Mary's explanation for this in *The Pioneer Policewoman* throws light on her view of the strengths developed by women involved in the suffrage movement:

> Their public work, including as it did, haranguing crowds at all seasons, in all neighbourhoods, under the most unfavourable conditions, had taught them how to face with astonishing courage and resolution the most virulent forms of opposition – howling derision or personal violence. If it did nothing else, this sharp discipline prepared them in the grimmest school of endurance for the urgent problems the war engendered, inculcating invaluable lessons in organisation, obedience, cheerfulness in adversity, fortitude and self-control. (p.13)

Although she was a suffragette for only five or six years, the experience shaped Mary as a woman who needed to lead others. Her next step took her to heights she had never imagined possible when she left home such a short time ago.

5

'POLLIES!'

The outbreak of war in 1914, and the cessation of suffragist hostilities, left Mary casting around for a new occupation. It was while travelling on a London bus that she heard people joking about women police, a conversation reconstructed in *Lady in Blue* with typical embellishment and attention to the most important detail – the uniform. '"Ladies in Blue!" exclaimed one with an uncontrollable chuckle. "Pollies! Fancy being run in by a pretty girl in a blue uniform and helmet!".'[1]

Mary was particularly keen to join a uniformed organisation, and a 'military' one: 'up to this time the only military body of women who were uniformed – (and a very smart uniform it was) – was known as the "Fanys" – First Aid Nursing Yeomanry.'[2] She chose not to volunteer for the FANYs, however: it may be that the work did not appeal to her, or that they required women of more robust health than Mary's. Delicate since her childhood, she had been further weakened by hunger strikes and forcible feeding while in Holloway Prison. But she was scornful of the more womanly role of organiser for Queen Mary's Needlework Guild, despite its splendid enamel badge. 'Without deprecating this excellent and necessary work, it seemed to my feverish energy a proposition almost as absurd as expecting a racehorse to draw a perambulator.'[3]

Mary discovered that a number of policing groups were being set up by women who saw an opportunity opening up for them with the deployment of men to the Front. Prominent among the trailblazers was Nina Boyle of the Women's Freedom League (a breakaway women's suffrage organisation whose members believed the WSPU to be excessively authoritarian). Nina Boyle, a journalist, had real anxieties about the monitoring of women's activities in wartime, since the Defence of the Realm Act (known as DORA) had been passed in the House of Commons on 8 August 1914 without debate. Under this Act, whose primary purpose was to prevent the publication of information of use to the enemy, the military authorities were given wide-reaching powers, including the control of civilian behaviour. Boyle was particularly afraid that the Contagious Diseases Acts of the 1860s – which enshrined in law the notion that women should be punished for immorality and forcibly treated for venereal disease, while the men with whom they consorted were tolerated – might be revived under DORA. In order to have some influence over the way in which women were policed, she offered to recruit women special constables in the Metropolitan Police area, but the Commissioner of Special Constabulary, Sir Edward Ward, turned her down.

Boyle heard that Margaret Damer Dawson, a friend of Sir Edward Henry, Commissioner of the Metropolitan Police, was making progress with her own Women Police Volunteers (WPV), and decided to join forces with her. She was not to know how willing Dawson's organisation would be to comply with the draconian wartime emergency measures against women, imposed by the authorities under DORA.

Margaret Damer Dawson was born in Sussex in 1874, the daughter of Richard Dawson and Agnes, Lady Walsingham. She was a woman of aristocratic background and independent means, with a house at 10 Cheyne Row, Chelsea (now marked with a plaque, reading simply 'Margaret Damer Dawson lived here'), and another home, Danehill, in Lympne, Kent. She was a talented musician, studying at the London Academy of Music, where she gained a Diploma and Gold Medal; and a campaigner for animal welfare and various feminist and philanthropic causes.

In 1911, Margaret Damer Dawson was sharing her home at Lauderdale Mansions, Paddington, with the two most prominent campaigners for animal welfare in England at the time: Countess Emilie Augusta Louise (Lizzy) Lind af Hageby and Leisa Schartau, both born in Sweden in the 1870s, who came to London together to study medicine at the London School of Medicine for Women. They claimed that experiments were carried out on living, unanaesthetised dogs, and published a book revealing their findings, *The Shambles of Science*, in 1903. This led to court cases and a national scandal (known as the Brown Dog affair) which lasted seven years, and led to the setting up of a royal commission on vivisection, and subsequent new legislation. A statue of the Brown Dog in Battersea Park, London, became the target of attacks, mostly by students. It was removed in 1910. A new statue, put up by the National Anti-Vivisection Society, replaced it in 1985. Lizzy Lind af Hageby settled in England, where she lived until her death in 1963. She was President of the London Spiritualist Alliance from 1935 to 1943, and believed herself to be in communication with Anna Kingsford, a famous Victorian anti-vivisectionist.

Margaret Damer Dawson was an indefatigable campaigner:

Slaughter-house reform was one of the things she fought for, and to be able to speak with first-hand evidence, she visited slaughter-houses at home and abroad. When she visited the first, to keep control of herself she took a camera and photographed the killing. When asked how she managed to stand the sights, she said, 'I just dug the heel of one foot into the instep of the other – and did not realise what had happened till I found my boot was full of blood.'[4]

Margaret Damer Dawson's work in animal protection was recognised with medals from the King of Denmark, and the Finnish Society for the Protection of Animals.

Mary claims, in *The Pioneer Policewoman*, that Margaret's frequent trips abroad in connection with her animal welfare work, 'brought [her] face to face with international social problems, especially those in which women and children were concerned,'[5] and that this, along with her work with Belgian refugees arriving in London, some of whom were allegedly spirited away by white slavers, was what inspired her to apply in August 1914 for permission to organise a corps of voluntary women police. As a member of the National Vigilance Association (NVA) and the Criminal Law Amendment Committee (CLAC), she took a keen interest in 'social purity': like Mary, and the many ex-suffragettes who joined the WPV, she saw protection of women from their own folly, and from the predations of men, as key elements in the emancipation of women. The aim of the social purity movement was to reform attitudes to sexual behaviour, and Margaret Damer Dawson believed that this could be achieved by creating a force of women police with the specific roles of repressing the activities of prostitutes, patrolling public parks and open spaces, and inspecting women's lodgings to ensure that they were free of immoral associations. Although Margaret Damer Dawson and other NVA/CLAC members also concerned themselves with the protection of women, their approach to policing by women was far more repressive than that of other organisations set up to monitor the welfare of women in wartime.

The government looked more kindly, however, on the voluntary patrols inaugurated by the National Union of Women Workers (NUWW) to carry out welfare work in areas close to military camps. The NUWW were approached by Scotland Yard in 1914, and asked to set up patrols known as Women Voluntary Patrols (WVP) in the Metropolitan Police area 'to work among the women and girls who were coming to London in increasing numbers to hang around the various army camps, parks, recruiting stations and railway terminals'.[6] The WVP was formalised in 1917, when Mrs Sofia Stanley was appointed supervisor of thirty-seven special patrols in London, which grew to fifty-five by the end of that year. They received a subsidy from the Metropolitan Police, which gave them the seal of official (police) approval. Volunteers were trained by the National Union of Women Patrols Committee. Recruits to these patrols were part-timers willing to work locally, entirely independent of the existing (male) police forces, and only for the duration of the war.

There was no question of these patrols having any formal connection with (male) police forces, nor did anyone envisage a long-term future for them. The honorary secretary of the Patrols Committee of the NUWW wrote to *The Times* on 3 October 1917, 'the voluntary patrols are neither police nor rescue workers, but true friends of the girls, in the deepest and holiest sense of the word'. However, she does point out that the 'women patrols have been employed by the Commissioner of Police as auxiliaries to the police': another indication of the commissioner's preference for the women patrols over the Women Police Volunteers. This, and the temporary status of the Women Voluntary Patrols, distinguished it from the Women Police Volunteers, which its leaders hoped would endure after the war. When at the end of the war official sanction for the WPV (now renamed the Women Police Service) was not forthcoming, the 1918–19 Report of the Women Police Service was scathing in its criticism of voluntary patrols:

> The demand for policewomen does not yet equal the supply. The raising of an entirely new force of Women Police Patrols by the newly appointed Commissioner of Metropolitan Police was undoubtedly felt as an injustice to those women who have given meritorious service in the difficult days of war, to say nothing of the extra expense to the country which would have been saved had the large Force of already trained and uniformed women been transferred … Excellent as was the work of those self-sacrificing ladies, it was far too restricted and irregular to lead to the wide development which lay in front of the paid and trained policewoman.[7]

Accounts in *Lady in Blue* of Mary's first impressions of Margaret Damer Dawson are brief but informative. 'She had remarkably diverse and contradictory gifts, was keenly interested in sport as well as in all the arts, an experienced Alpine climber, an expert motorist, an enthusiastic gardener, a passionate lover of animals.' (p.8) Her physical appearance was 'blonde, blue-eyed, of a delicate complexion'. (p.10) In *The Pioneer Policewoman*, Mary wrote, 'Danger steeled her; she was encouraged, even inspired by difficulties'. This was a woman after Mary's own heart; a woman she could love. Mary describes Dawson's work with Belgian refugees ('that piteous invasion'), and the 'confidence-tricksters, pilferers, and to an even greater degree white slavers', who preyed on them. (pp.9–10) 'In order to combat these undesirables, Miss Damer Dawson decided to organise a body of Women Police, if possible with official recognition from the authorities. It was at this stage of affairs that I went to her, burning with anxiety to join the projected organisation.' (*Lady in Blue*, p.27)

It seems that the two women had not met before. Again Mary is succinct: 'The meeting between Margaret Damer Dawson and myself struck an immediate spark, and began a period – all too short, alas – of close association and intimate friendship, ending only with the sudden death of the Chief in 1920.'[8] This was indeed a close friendship: Mary lived with Margaret until her death, at which she was present, and inherited the whole of her estate under a will made in 1915, only a few months after they first met. Mary continued to live at Danehill, the home they had shared, until after the Second World War, although she owned numerous other properties, including a flat in London.

Meetings of the emerging WPV were held at Dawson's house at 10 Cheyne Row, and at St Stephen's House, Westminster, the first headquarters of the WPV. Among the volunteers who were enrolled were 'Mrs Meeson Coates, Miss St John Partridge, Miss E.F. Harburn, Miss I. Goldingham, my sister Mrs Hampton, Miss Olive Walton, Miss J.M. Campbell, and myself'.[9] Most of these women were former suffragettes, and all were mature women: at 36, Mary was the youngest.

According to Mary, the women drawn to Margaret Damer Dawson's burgeoning organisation were, 'mentally and physically above the average'. They were certainly privileged women of means, which perhaps is what she meant. There were also a number of talented women artists who already enjoyed independent lives and sought to promote women's capabilities. Dora Meeson Coates, an Australian designer of stained glass, was a member of the Artists' Suffrage League (ASL) formed in January 1907, as was Annie St John Partridge. The ASL created propaganda materials, including banners, posters, postcards and Christmas cards. Another notable ex-suffragette was Olive Walton, a WSPU organiser, who had been imprisoned for window-breaking. She was famously photographed being arrested in Dundee in 1914 when she tried to throw a petition into the king's carriage during a royal visit to the city.

Some of those named by Mary remained as stalwarts in the organisation: Miss J.M. Campbell, who rose to the rank of chief inspector; Ellen Harburn; Isobel Goldingham; and Dolly Hampton.

Ellen Frances Harburn was born Haarbleicher. She made several donations to the WSPU under this name, but she changed her name to Harburn when anti-German feeling became prevalent in Britain at the beginning of the war. She had been a school manager with the London County Council, worked in special schools for the deaf, and set up girls' and women's clubs, and a travelling library scheme.

Isobel Frances Goldingham, a former WSPU hunger striker, was born in India in 1874 to an army family. She became a driving force within the WPV, and a close friend of Mary for many years: they were still in touch in the 1930s.

Margaret ('Dolly') Hampton, Mary Allen's sister, had been married for some years, and was the mother of two young children when she joined the WPV. She was the only one of this initial group who continued to work as a policewoman under the auspices of the Metropolitan Police, appointed by them in May 1915 to serve at the London borough of Richmond.

Mary explains in *The Pioneer Policewoman* why so many ex-suffragettes were attracted to police work:

> Their efforts – whether rightly or wrongly exercised is fortunately no longer in question – had not only shaken vast numbers of women out of their normal indifference to political questions, but had brought some of them into close, sometimes painful touch with the police, teaching them how very unpleasant it is for an alleged woman culprit to be handled by men. In the course of the long-protracted struggle they had gone through a severe novitiate. (p.13)

There is a suggestion of regret here at Mary's own militant past ('if it did nothing else'); but it is clear that she saw police work as the ideal continuation of the suffragists' mission to bring about a permanent change in women's roles in society, using the skills learned in the years leading up to the outbreak of war in 1914. However, these qualifications were precisely what the authorities objected to most. Mary herself was willing to forgive and forget past encounters with the police, but her militant background and her criminal record did not endear her to the Metropolitan Police, who were to find more amenable recruits for their own official women's police force after the war among the members of the NUWW's voluntary patrols.

The only precedent for women in policing before the outbreak of the First World War was a loose system of police matrons. These women were often the wives of police officers who lived in or very near to the police station. They were recruited to care for the interests of women in custody, and their children. This was a voluntary duty, and an accepted part of the lot of a station sergeant's wife, who would also be expected to feed the station's complement of officers and any prisoners in the cells.

Some female police officers were already in place before the war, appointed by local police authorities which, although nominally under the control of the Home Office, enjoyed considerable autonomy. On 3 April 1914, it was reported in *Votes for Women* that:

> The first English policewoman has been appointed in Liverpool in the person of Mrs Hughes, who, as 'police inspector', will have a commission to protect the interests of children in the city … Although policewomen have not yet been appointed in this country, the movement in their favour goes ahead … We have no information regarding her salary, but we hope Mrs Hughes has insisted on being given the salary that a man inspector of her grade now receives.

There was some support in government circles for official recognition of policewomen: 'We agree with Sir William Byles [one of the MPs who joined Mary Allen and Keir Hardie in the inspection of Holloway on 13 August 1909]. The argument in favour of policewomen, he said, was absolutely unanswerable.'[10] But this was insufficient to impress the Metropolitan Police hierarchy – a highly influential law unto themselves.

The WPV pressed on, despite no formal acknowledgement of their potential usefulness, or even of their existence. Mary states in *The Pioneer Policewoman* that Sir Edward Henry, Chief Commissioner of Police, gave Margaret Damer Dawson 'permission to form a corps of Women Police Volunteers to work in the Metropolitan area,' in August 1914. (p.23) She fails to mention an earlier rebuff, described by Margaret in a speech in October 1916: 'two and a half years ago, when they were begging Sir Edward Henry to allow them to work on the streets, he shook his head and said, "You will get yourselves knocked on the head, and you surely don't expect me to look after a lot of women".'[11] It was actually Nina Boyle and not Margaret Dawson, who headed the organisation at the time of Sir Edward Henry's initial refusal to allow women a policing role. Mary's error cannot be ascribed to forgetfulness: she always paid close attention to accurate detail; but for Mary, the WPV was always and only the brainchild of Margaret Damer Dawson.

Sir Edward Henry, formerly of the Indian Civil Service and Inspector General of Police in Bengal, was Commissioner of Police of the Metropolis from 1903 to 1918. He is remembered as an innovative commissioner, introducing police dogs, typewriters, telephones and fingerprinting to the force. In 1912, he survived an attempt on his life by a cab driver, whose licence had been refused. Three shots were fired, one of them entering his abdomen. He resigned his position as commissioner in 1918 when the government, in his absence and against his wishes, gave in to the demands of striking police officers. He was succeeded by Sir Nevil Macready.

After Sir Edward Henry gave the go-ahead to the WPV in 1914, Nina Boyle was still in charge. On 26 February 1915, *Votes for Women* reported:

We are informed that Miss Nina Boyle is now Chief of the Women Police Volunteers. The work of the Corps proceeds on the following lines: (1) To keep a uniformed woman on duty in every park, garden and common throughout the London area during the summer months, and (2) to have an officer on duty in every police court all the year round. The Corps has abandoned all emergency work, in connection with military centres, or elsewhere, in favour of concentrating on work in connection with the criminal courts, a form of activity with which we, who have so often shown in these columns the evil effects of the absence of women from such places, have every sympathy.

(It was also noted that 'A special section for the protection of animals is in the process of formation', although this seems not to have materialised.)

The *Votes for Women* article may have been part of a last attempt by Nina Boyle to retain control. Her days as chief of the Women Police Volunteers were numbered: inevitably, given the disagreements between herself and Margaret Damer Dawson about the nature of their role. Boyle believed that the prosecution of only *criminal* behaviour by women should be in their remit, and that it was against women's interests to police their morals. Dawson, on the other hand, was happy to comply with any restrictions on women's movements ordered by chief constables. It was because of this authoritarian stance that, in February 1915, Nina Boyle asked Margaret Damer Dawson to resign from her position of deputy chief. Margaret promptly called a meeting of the whole corps of fifty policewomen. All but two took her part. She thereupon formed the Women Police Service (WPS), which effectively put Nina Boyle's initiative at an end. By August

1917, the WPS had 560 uniformed women at work in those areas where chief constables were willing to employ them.*

❧❧❧

The aims and objectives of the WPS were to help women and children, and to keep them safe from men and from themselves. Margaret Damer Dawson sincerely believed that 'there was no place more dangerous for the British child than the public park, and it was not safe to allow a small girl to stray more than a few yards alone, for these places were haunted by men with criminal tendencies'.[12] Mary was equally concerned at the effects of war and, in particular, the absence of men:

> The gradual dislocation of all the public services, through the indiscrimi-
> nate enlistment of men; the concentration of huge numbers of these raw
> recruits in training camps; the fever of excitement in the very air … cre-
> ated new and pressing problems with which it was clear the existing police
> force could never cope unaided … The very children were thrown off
> their balance by the pervading atmosphere of excitement, confusion and
> unrest, as well as by the absence from home of the family disciplinarian.[13]

There was considerable support for the idea of women police, and for the WPS in particular, from the *British Journal of Nursing* (BJN), a weekly pub-lication with a large readership among nurses and other women's groups. Most of its articles were written by the editor, Mrs Bedford Fenwick, a woman who used her journal as a platform for the expression of her own strong views. She believed that trained nurses were particularly suitable for police work and, in the 27 June 1914 edition of the BJN, she wrote about the humanity of women as opposed to the 'brute force' of male constables, and the difficulty for women in approaching male officers for advice, particularly as some had, 'misled girls into bad houses. The woman police officer in uni-form will be a light-house preventing in some cases the wrecking of a life.'

All WPS volunteers were trained, initially at St Stephen's House, Westminster, in first aid, drill, self-defence (ju-jitsu), police court procedure

---

* All these initials are confusing. To clarify: the women police force had three names in
succession. The Women Police Volunteers (WPV) was formed in 1914 by Nina Boyle
and Margaret Damer Dawson. In February 1915, Margaret Damer Dawson took over
and renamed it as the Women Police Service (WPS). After a court case in 1921, by
which time Mary Allen was in charge, the name was changed to Women's Auxiliary
Service (WAS).

and signalling. 'We learned our technique and got acquainted with the regulations by borrowing all the textbooks we could obtain that dealt with the
work of men police.'[14] The curriculum during the four weeks' training was
demanding and varied, including psychology, police court procedure, police
law, children's courts, factories, social conditions, as well as drill and patrols.
Mary's sister, Inspector Hampton, a probation officer with the Richmond
police, was a visiting lecturer. Mary was deeply involved with the recruit-
ment process: 'During the course of training an oral examination is held
by Commandant Allen, who makes a point of individual questioning, thus
coming into personal contact with each Recruit.'[15] Later, additional training
schools were established in Bristol and Edinburgh.

Funding was entirely voluntary at first: many recruits were what Mary
called, 'women of leisure',[16] but even their resources were inadequate to
fulfil the ambitious aims of the WPS. 'Half a dozen pioneers started with
£5 as their total funds',[17] and Margaret Damer Dawson worked hard at sup-
plementing the bank account by addressing meetings of likely supporters.
'It was not till 1916 that the Government made the Women Police Service
a grant; but it never sufficed to free us from financial anxieties.'[18] An anony-
mous donor did, however, provide a sum large enough to enable the WPS
to move to larger premises at Little George Street, Westminster. This person
is referred to in the 1918–19 Report:

> The Women Police Service is financed by one donor, who has devoted
> the fortunes left by her two sons who fell in the war to the purpose of
> promoting the work of women police. This donor wishes still to remain
> anonymous. Women police of the present and the future owe a very deep
> meed of gratitude to the donor who has been watching over the devel-
> opment of the movement, taking the keenest interest in the work being
> done and withholding nothing which a generous heart and head could
> foresee as a need which financial help could meet.[19]

The identity of this benefactor was revealed in a court case in April 1930
as Anne Maria Trouton, the wife of the Irish physicist Frederick Thomas
Trouton. She first met Margaret Damer Dawson in 1916, and became
an ardent supporter of the WPS. Two of her sons were killed in the First
World War: Eric in 1915 and Desmond in 1917. She made a will on 28 May
1920, leaving a large legacy to the WAS (formerly WPS). When she died
on 27 October 1929, by this time a widow, she left an estate of £55,000.
Her two surviving sons, Rupert de Burgh Trouton, economist, broker and
whaler; and Maurice, an inventor, contested the 1920 will, and produced

a will dated 16 July 1909, which left everything to her two sons and three daughters. Rupert claimed that his mother was not of sound mind on 28 May 1920, when she left money to the WPS, and that she did not know or approve of the contents. Two doctors examined her in January 1921, and one gave evidence that in his opinion she was not fit to make a will in May 1920. 'The loss of two sons killed in the War had had a very great effect on the testatrix's health ... She purported to give away large sums of money at a time when she had not got the money to give.'

It was stated in court that Commandant Allen 'never for one moment wished to insist on the will if it were made by a woman of unsound mind who was not fit to make it, though they were anxious to do their duty by the service'. The judge pronounced for the earlier will, and said that 'the Women's Auxiliary Service were well advised to take the course which they had, and had behaved very properly in the circumstances'.[20] However, the loss of this very important legacy was a bitter blow.

❧❧

At last Mary had an opportunity to wear a uniform and have a hand in its design. She had worn the suffragette colours of white, green and gold, with pride; but there had been no standardisation: women wore whatever they had to hand. Mary wanted a military style for the WPS, with badges of rank and plenty of leather.

Margaret Damer Dawson submitted a design to Sir Edward Henry in August 1914 and, having received his approval, uniformed policewomen started to appear on the streets of London the following month. 'It was a very simple, business-like garb, dark blue, plainly cut, with shoulder straps bearing at first WPV, afterwards WPS in silver letters. With a hard felt hat to complete their costume, the new members of the force were chiefly conspicuous for their sober neatness.' Mary was convinced of the deterrent effectiveness of a uniform, which had 'a prompt moral effect' – so much so, that a modified version was later adopted by the Women Patrols.[21] In 1917, senior officers had a new design ('officers wore a flat cap with silver braid'), both to distinguish them from the lower ranks, and to allow senior officers to ride a fleet of motorcycles. With the purchase of these new machines, Mary was able to justify the unprecedented wearing of boots and trousers.

In 1916, a New Zealander called Bessie Spencer (Anna Elizabeth Jerome Spencer) went to London to look for suitable war work. She visited the headquarters of the WPS, where she met Dorothy Pethick, younger sister of Emmeline Pethick-Lawrence, the suffragette friend and colleague of Mary

Allen. Miss Pethick was a sergeant in the WPS, and through her, Bessie met Margaret Damer Dawson and Mary Allen. Bessie described these 'charming women', describing Margaret Damer Dawson as 'almost small and very neat and trim' and Mary, who was 'aggressively uniformed' with 'the utmost aversion for dresses', wearing 'peaked hat, navy-blue breeches, knee-high shiny black boots and monocle'.[22]

Photographs of Mary and Margaret taken during the war show us the image they wished to project. The uniform makes no concession to femininity, and it is substantially identical to that worn by the armed forces. With their cropped hair, the two women could easily be mistaken for men: an intentional mistake. It has been noted by Emily Hamer that:

> Before the mid-1920s the only way a middle-class woman stood any chance of wearing clothes which were not feminine, let alone trousers, was by wearing a uniform. Belonging to an organization such as the WPS which required members to wear a military-style uniform gave to the watching heterosexual world a justification of why a woman was wearing men's clothes … Uniforms gave lesbians visibility without putting them in position of danger, for they also explicitly provided a reason for wearing men's clothes – membership of a particular group – which was not simply lesbianism. Given this, it is not surprising that lesbians had more than sartorial reasons for preferring to help the war effort via uniformed work rather than by knitting.[23]

The image projected by the WPS uniform was a cause of unease to the (male) police authorities, who were bewildered and offended in equal measure by the overt masculinity of Mary Allen and the majority of her senior colleagues. But the uniform was to become contentious for quite another reason, when the WPS was charged, after the end of the war, with masquerading as Metropolitan policewomen, who wore a uniform almost identical to that designed by and for the WPS.

Mary and Margaret Damer Dawson were determined to use the opportunities presented by war to promote women's policing. They had two pieces of good fortune – although, like all good luck, it was mostly the result of hard work. The first was an invitation to work in Grantham, a small Lincolnshire town with a sudden influx of army troops and the concomitant camp followers. The second was an unprecedented expansion of munitions factories, whose huge female workforce required some sort of policing.

6

On Actual Police Duty

'The first employment of women in uniform *on actual police duty* was late in November 1914.'[1]

In 1914, Grantham, a small market town in Lincolnshire which concerned itself almost exclusively with farming and hunting, had a population of 20,000. This number nearly doubled when thousands of troops moved in to the newly established Machine Gun Training Centre at Belton Park, just outside the town. The attendant problems posed by this influx of men are summed up by Mary in *Lady in Blue*:

> A serious problem was provided by numbers of workless or unstable girls who hung about the outskirts of the camp. They were in no sense of the word criminals; often they were simply carried away in an hysteria of patriotism, and wished to give something – anything, even themselves – to the men who were so shortly going out to fight for England, and who perhaps in many cases might never taste happiness again. (pp.29–30)

These words, written more than twenty years later, show Mary in an unusually sympathetic light. She had very little time for prostitutes, but she appears to view the presence of young women hanging around the camp as a form of selfless war work, although she must have known that a proportion of these unfortunate women were actually earning a living in the only way open to them.

Margaret Damer Dawson's brother-in-law, Staff Captain Kensington,* suggested that his commanding officer, Brigadier-General Hammersley,

---

* Edgar Claude Kensington married Margaret's sister, Katherine Damer Dawson, in 1907.

approach the WPV for help in controlling the large number of camp
followers. There was no mechanism by which policewomen could be paid
from the rates (as was the case for policemen), but a voluntary committee,
the Association for the Help and Care of Girls, was set up in Grantham by
Lady Thorold to fund two policewomen.

Mary claims that she was afraid of being selected to go to Grantham,
and that she absented herself from headquarters in the hope of being
overlooked. This is unusually coy: Mary was always eager for action, and
would normally welcome the opportunity of being chosen. It is possible that her fledgling relationship with Margaret Damer Dawson was
the real reason for her reluctance to leave London. Whatever the truth of
this, Margaret:

> with the courage of a true leader* ... summoning me, her second in com-
> mand, as well as Miss E.F. Harburn, crisply informed us that we were to be
> detached forthwith for this special work ... The first valiant policewomen
> in embryo departed in a state of the deadliest funk.[2]

Mary and Ellen Harburn left London by train on 27 November 1914,
accompanied by Margaret Damer Dawson. They all wore their uniforms,
which Mary felt made them 'terribly conspicuous'. Arriving in rainy
Grantham they, 'splashed through mud puddles towards our lodgings,
noting with sinking hearts a general aspect of squalor'.[3] Margaret Damer
Dawson stayed for a few days, helping them to get to know the area, and
plan their activities.

A photograph was printed in the 19 December 1914 edition of the
Grantham Journal under the heading: 'Women Police for Grantham Streets:
Enterprising Move by Local Association.' Mary and Ellen Harburn, nervous
and unsmiling, stand either side of a seated Margaret Damer Dawson, who
appears frail and distant, looking away from the camera. The caption under
the photograph reads:

> The Local Officers. The Grantham Association for the Help and Care
> of Girls have deemed it advisable for the protection and guidance of
> local young women to introduce lady police-officers into the town. As
> our snapshot indicates, they are attired in a neat uniform, and they com-
> menced their patrol duties on Wednesday night.

---

* At the end of 1914, Nina Boyle was actually the leader of the WPV. Mary chooses to
ignore this fact. Margaret Damer Dawson became leader in February 1915.

A further report in the *Grantham Journal* states that:

> The first women police officers to patrol the streets of any town north of London made their appearance at Grantham on Wednesday, when their presence aroused considerable interest. They have come at the instigation of the Association for the Help and Care of Girls, on account of the large number of troops camped in the vicinity of the town, the idea being that trained women could effect more good in keeping girls and young women from evil influences than inexperienced persons. The Corps of Women Police Volunteers, from which the members at present working in Grantham have been drawn, was enrolled with the object of providing a body of trained women for the service of the public. Instruction has been given in drill, signalling, first aid, self defence, procedure at Police-courts, and the method of collecting accurate information, and the duties, in short, are about identical with those of present police-constables. A smart uniform of navy blue is worn by all women police when on duty, and a felt hat somewhat similar to an ordinary bowler hat. Strict discipline is maintained, and authority is vested in a chief and assistant chiefs. The Chief of the Corps, Miss Damer Dawson, who has come to Grantham to supervise the preliminary work of the women police, informs the 'Journal' that the organisation has been started in a spirit of earnest and responsible endeavour, and not with a view to sensational effect or amateur effort.

Mary and Margaret are putting down markers for the future. This is no passing phenomenon. As far as they are concerned, women police are here to stay.

Mary soon discovered that there was no formal supervision or control of the troops once they were outside the camp perimeter, although the area was under 'partial martial law'. The military police, who had superseded the ordinary constabulary and were in effect the employers of the two women, seemed unsure what to do with them, beyond instructing them to keep an eye on ill-lit alleys, courts, yards and passages. Mary observed that their brief, 'to see to it that the twenty thousand military did not get themselves into trouble', gave them 'only about ten thousand apiece', to watch.[4]

Ellen Harburn was given the responsibility of 'public-house duty'.[5] Mary reported that, on entering her first public house, Ellen Harburn found the publican more frightened than she was. Their training in ju-jitsu came in handy when a strong arm was needed, but Mary is at pains to stress that they were universally welcomed and respected. Silence fell when they marched into a public house, but, 'it was not long before we were consulted by anxious parents in regard to their sons and daughters; by young girls, culprits or victims; by street women not too hardened to hope for better things'.[6] Both military and civil police became increasingly friendly, and Lady Thorold gave continued support. More women police were drafted in from London to help.

The ethical problems foreseen by Nina Boyle were quick to arise. The military authorities granted to the two policewomen 'the right to enter any house, building or land within a six-mile radius of the Army Post Office'.[7] Early in 1915, General Hammersley imposed a curfew on 'women of loose character' in Grantham, between six o'clock at night and seven in the morning. This measure, which was intended to discourage prostitution, was in effect a reintroduction of police powers under the Contagious Diseases Act, and Mary Allen and Ellen Harburn were willingly enforcing it. In fact, they were paid by Lady Thorold's committee, and not by the military, so that, in choosing to do General Hammersley's bidding, the WPV were making their own moral judgement, interpreting Hammersley's undefined 'women of loose character' as they saw fit:

> It was the two officers' uninhibited exercise of these and other emergency powers to 'go into women's houses and to see if the girls were in bed and … who was in the house,' conduct searches and inspections of billets and hostelries and expel 'hundreds' of suspected wrongdoers in the course of their public morality campaign that led to an open confrontation between Boyle and Dawson over the WPVs methods early in 1915.[8]

There can be little doubt that Mary Allen and Margaret Damer Dawson were more anxious to serve the interests of the men who directed police and military activities than they were to support their own sex. The women they dealt with in Grantham were regarded by them almost as a separate species: shiftless girls and hardened prostitutes. They envisaged an authoritative force of policewomen led by educated and relatively wealthy women whose role was to control and exert power over women and children. With the demise of Nina Boyle, Allen and Dawson were in a position to pursue their own shared agenda. They saw their wartime activities as a prelude to a permanent force of women police and a test of their abilities. Mary's ambition is clear when she notes that Grantham 'provided an infinite variety of opportunities to "acquire merit"'.[9]

Mary's excitement overcame her fear in Grantham, despite the inherent dangers of the work. White slavery was always at the back of her mind. Before entering a house while searching for missing soldiers, she turned to her companion: "'How do we know," I demanded, "that we shall ever be permitted to come out again?" Lurid tales of the disappearance of women flashed into our minds.'[10] The idea that any white slaver would abduct a 36-year-old woman with cropped hair and a military-style uniform, is comical, but surely unintentionally so. But there can be no doubt that real physical danger attended their work, although Mary underplays the risks they ran by her use of trivialising language:

> It was a trying time for Miss Harburn and myself when, after perhaps twelve or fourteen hours of unceasing duty, we came upon a street-fight in which a couple of big factory girls were engaged tooth and nail, surrounded by jeering and cheering crowds of onlookers, and we had to straighten out the tangle.[11]

General Hammersley expressed his appreciation of the services of Mary and Ellen Harburn in a letter to the chief of the WPV (still Nina Boyle at this point) dated 14 January 1915. He had heard that they might be removed, which was true – their experience was needed elsewhere – although they were to be replaced by other women. Miss Teed and Mrs Smith were adopted by the Town Council as members of the local police force. They, 'retained the uniform of the Women Police Service ... but exchanged the cap badge for the Arms of Grantham', and were, 'sworn in and paid out of police funds in the same way as men, and working directly under the orders of the Chief Constable'.[12] Miss Teed is not heard of again, but Edith Smith, a qualified nurse, was given full powers of arrest, and received pay above that given to male constables, in recognition of the long hours she worked and her devotion to duty. She lived 'on the premises' (presumably at the police station), had no days off, no overtime pay, and no provision for a pension. The long hours took their toll: Edith, the first officially recognised woman police officer in Britain, only lasted two years in the job; five years after leaving the force she died of a morphine overdose. She is remembered in Grantham, with a display in the museum, and a short stretch of road in the town centre named after her.

Mary and Ellen Harburn were transferred to Hull, leaving in May 1915, accompanied by Margaret Damer Dawson, the Chief. The Bishop of Hull had persuaded the borough council to request two WPV policewomen. However much the Bishop may have welcomed them, it is tempting to speculate on the reaction of the existing Women Patrols to Mary's arrival: 'We had at once to organise and control a body of forty women patrols already on the spot, but who had been working more or less in the dark, with no definite or practical leadership.'[13] Clearly she regarded these women as amateurs, much in need of her professional direction. Her use of the revealing word 'control' sums up her attitude to those she regards as undisciplined outsiders.

Hull presented new challenges, and in particular the effects of air raids. Mary recalls the sight of an airship – a Zeppelin – hovering over the town on the night of Sunday, 5 June, and describes her feeling of terror at seeing in reality what she had only before seen in newspaper illustrations. The horror of the bombing raids that followed impressed Mary deeply, and amidst the noise and dust she tried to help the injured and get them to cars which would take them to hospital. She gives warm praise in *The Pioneer Policewoman* and in *Lady in Blue* to the work of Dr Mary Murdoch, a forthright ex-suffragette who became a surgeon at the children's hospital in Hull, and Hull's first GP. Mary Murdoch regularly appeared after air raids, giving first aid, and using her own car to transport the wounded.

During the bombing raids, Mary was struck by the effects of panic:

The unfortunate inhabitants of the poorer districts would seize the first objects at hand – piling up their possessions in the family perambulator, from under which it was sometimes necessary to rescue half-smothered babies. As a consequence the parks were littered with large framed pictures, birds in cages, huge vases, sea-shells, bundles of clothing, bedding, and the most incongruous and astonishing articles.[14]

'In one house, the family was hiding pathetically under a double-bed. When they heard my boots on the stairs, someone screamed; I think they thought the German invaders had landed.'[15] Given Mary's severe military appearance, perhaps their fears had some justification. With increasingly frequent air raids people took to sleeping outside in the open, where the imposition of the 'lighting order' made total darkness an additional hazard.

The duties of the two policewomen were generally and non-specifically to keep order, which they interpreted as patrolling public houses and fried fish shops. They were expected to attend the police court in the Town Hall where, as women, they were far from welcome. It was traditional to eject women from the court from time to time, when delicate matters were under discussion. Mary and Miss Harburn firmly ignored the cry of 'All females out of court' and, after appealing to the chief constable on the matter, they were eventually allowed to stay.

Five WPV officers served in Hull until 1918. They were never sworn in, but were permitted to arrest drunk and disorderly women 'for their own protection'.[16]

Mary was undoubtedly relieved when she was summoned back to London to become involved in training the large number of new recruits who were now in demand for work in munitions factories and army camps all over the country.

ॐ

Despite the difficulties inherent in working with those male police officers who saw no point in women police, Mary found them to be generally friendly and helpful; particularly the higher ranks, as we might expect given her regard for hierarchies: 'the Inspectors ... as soon as they realised that their female colleagues were prepared to salute them with becoming gravity, and to treat them in every way with due respect, were equally inclined to cordial relations.'[17] Mary had felt the same when on the other side of the law: as a suffragette, she said, 'the police were our protectors far more than they were ever our adversaries'.[18]

Mary liked men; her own father was kind and generous, if a little strict, and she remembered him with affection. The enemies she made tended to be women who opposed her, rather than men who stood in her way. It is unlikely that the police constables were quite as chivalrous as Mary suggests, 'ready to help, but never to interfere',[19] but she was unfailingly generous and forgiving in her writing towards those men who presented no real threat to her ambition.

ॐ

Mary's sister, Christine Duncan (later Sandeman) became a member of the Women Police Service in Edinburgh in 1915, when her daughters were very young. Christine is almost certainly the woman described in *Lady in Blue* (pp.38–9) who was trained and supplied at the request of the Admiralty in 1916:

> for anti-espionage work, and to help to tackle the problem of the drug traffic, which was then growing to very dangerous proportions among soldiers back on leave from the Front ... Our unit disguised herself as a prostitute, got to know all her supposed colleagues, moved in circles where she was in constant extreme danger from drug-runners, and

obtained information of a most important kind, both in connection with drug-running and spying.

Christine was an adventurous woman, bored by an unsuccessful marriage to a man twenty years her senior. She would undoubtedly have been prepared to take risks: indeed she did so throughout her life. In Edinburgh she worked as a welfare officer, helping out women who had been released from prison, and accommodating them in the family home. Christine's daughter, Bunty, wrote: 'My sister and I had a wonderful upbringing as our house was full of mother's criminals, who came to tea.'[20] Mary praises her magnificent work, which apparently prevented 'serious naval loss' through the activities of a notorious female German spy, Lizzie Wertheim.

The Women Police Service became an efficient organisation, thanks to the co-operation of the three women who ran it: the Council of Three, as Mary called them. Margaret Damer Dawson was in overall charge of policy; Mary implemented that policy; and Isobel Goldingham took care of administration. In line with other women's groups doing their bit in wartime, they modelled themselves on the active fighting troops. 'To draw a military comparison, Miss Damer Dawson was Commander-in-Chief, I was in command of the actual field of battle, while Miss Isobel Goldingham was in command of the staff.'[21] Unlike the FANYs and other women's services, the leaders of the WPS looked forward to a time 'when policewomen in particular should be recognised not merely as an emergency organisation, but as an integral part of the world system of maintaining law and order'.[22] With her customary zeal, Mary was already thinking in terms of an international force of women police.

As we have seen, Mary and Margaret Damer Dawson had developed an intimate relationship shortly after the outbreak of war. The third member of the WPS triumvirate was Isobel Goldingham, known to Mary from her suffrage days. Isobel Goldingham was a woman of independent means, born in India, the daughter of an Indian civil servant, 'from whom she perhaps inherited her unusually precise and judicial turn of mind'.[23] A tall, masculine woman, she was to remain among Mary's close friends for many years. These three strong-minded women were the backbone of the WPS, whose force of character as individuals combined to make them an efficient machine when their services were called upon.

As the WPS grew, it became necessary to regularise the arrangements for policewomen's pay, which came from a variety of sources: local committees, local rates, and voluntary contributions. Mary and Margaret approached Herbert Samuel, the Home Secretary, who introduced a clause into the police, factories etc. (Miscellaneous) Provisions Act of July 1916, which brought women's pay into line with that of policemen. The urgency of this change arose from the second fortuitous invitation to provide police-women: this time from the Ministry of Munitions.

❧❀❧

The Ministry of Munitions of War was established under the leadership of Lloyd George in March 1915 to address the growing problem of muni-tions shortages affecting front line British troops in Europe. Large numbers of women were being employed to meet the sudden demand for weap-onry, and those women needed supervision on security grounds, as well as to keep them from becoming unruly. Mary gives different accounts of the WPS initial involvement in munitions factories: in *Lady in Blue* she writes of a personal interview with Lloyd George, who 'expressed himself thor-oughly satisfied with our work, and made several tentative suggestions for widening its scope (pp.40–41); in *The Pioneer Policewoman*[24] it is Sir Edward Henry who recommends the WPS to the ministry. This seems more likely, given Henry's earlier support for the WPS; 'tentative suggestions' from a man as confident and assertive as Lloyd George are inconceivable.

The WPS responded to a request from the Ministry of Munitions to provide policewomen to work in factories and munitions areas by putting the whole of their organisation at the ministry's disposal. Mary returned to London after a short period of service at Hull to train recruits, now needed in increasingly large numbers. As part of her duties, she travelled the country, monitoring standards and the changing needs for women police, and taking part in inspections by royalty, which gave her the greatest satisfaction. On one occasion, when Queen Alexandra was visiting a munitions factory, the queen dropped a glove in front of Mary who, having stood to attention for three hours while waiting for the royal party, was too stiff to bend down and pick it up. It is hard to believe in the folly of any group of women standing to attention for three hours; but whatever the truth of this, Mary goes on to relate an even more extraordinary incident: 'Then Queen Alexandra did one of those kindly things for which she was notable. "Please do not move!" she commanded me gently. "I have a new shooting stick here, and I wish to pick it up on that myself if I can." And she did so with instant dexterity.'[25]

This is Mary showing us, albeit unconsciously, that she is as good as the next woman, even if that next woman is a queen. Not only does she omit to pick up the glove, she is actually doing Queen Alexandra a favour in letting it lie on the ground.

Extraordinarily, the WPS entered into a contract with the Ministry of Munitions in April 1916 to train and equip ten women on a six-month trial basis *without any payment.* This put an intolerable strain on their finances, which relied on donations and the personal funds of the better-off members and, at the end of the year, they appealed to the ministry for a grant for salaries and office expenses. Margaret Damer Dawson and Mary Allen had signed agreements with the ministry on 7 July 1916 (to provide and supervise policewomen at HM Queen's Ferry Factory) and on 31 October 1916 (the same for HM Factory Gretna), and also provided women police at the factories at Waltham Abbey and Pembrey. Only in an agreement signed on 26 January 1917 was payment to the WPS and a pay structure for their members formalised. On the same day, an advertisement appeared in *The Times* under the headline 'Women Police Wanted':

> The Ministry of Munitions has need of several hundred policewomen to take up police posts in his Majesty's factories, and the Minister has appointed Miss Damer Dawson, Chief Officer, and Miss M. S. Allen, Chief Superintendent, of the Women Police Service as agents to supply women for this work. The Women Police Service offers the necessary training, and this, which takes place in London, occupies three weeks. An allowance is granted during training and good salaries are offered on appointment. Three hundred women are wanted immediately.

Under this agreement, recruits were to be paid 25*s* per week during the one month's training, unless the minister was satisfied that this sum was insufficient, 'owing to the class of the recruit engaged or proposed to be engaged,'[26] in which case it could be increased to a sum not exceeding 30*s* per week. Once in post, chief inspectors were to receive payment of £3 per week; inspectors £2 10*s*; sergeants £2 5*s*; and ordinary policewomen £2. These sums were very small,* and uniforms were to be provided and maintained by the officers at their own expense. In addition, from 1 January 1917, the ministry would repay salaries of headquarters' staff up to a maximum

---

* In 1915, 25*s* had the spending power of about £115 today (2012); in 1920 its value had fallen to about half that amount.

sum of £850 per annum (roughly equivalent to £40,000 in 2012). This sum (called a grant in the 1918–19 WPS Report) was doubled in January 1918.

The work undertaken by the WPS in the munitions factories was extremely exacting and dangerous: their duties included patrolling the factories, canteens and nearby towns; general policing of petty crime; and searching women for smuggled items such as cigarettes and hairpins, which were strictly forbidden in the vicinity of high explosives. In addition, there was the constant danger from air raids, which involved rapid safe evacuation of premises. Mary praises highly the women who worked in the WPS uniform for their courage and devotion to duty; and, never forgetting the importance of middle-class standards, she believes that they had a moderating effect on the young women under supervision: 'The conversation among the workers had been frequently appallingly coarse, young girls of nineteen and twenty using the most profane language. Continued remonstrances, grave but kindly, were in the end effectual, and in consequence the whole tone of the factory was raised.'[27]

Mary was particularly concerned about the effect on young women of having money of their own which, 'drove them to feverish excitements or extravagances and, coupled with their anxiety and loneliness, often to drink; so that some of them sank, during the four years of their freedom from all supervision, to a terrible and often scarcely human condition'.[28] Given the strict supervision imposed by the WPS in the munitions factories, this seems hardly fair. Once again, we see, 'evidence of the primacy of class interests over gender solidarity during the war. That these groups of organised feminists, who sought to open the career of policing to women, were prepared to use women of the working class as objects for their own ends was a harsh assertion of their priorities.'[29]

Mary's obsession with morality, and the role of middle- and upper-class women in controlling it, is equalled by her ignorance of some basic facts. She writes in *The Pioneer Policewoman* that, 'recent investigation has made it clear that diseases consequent on vice are more readily acquired and transmitted by young girls just entering upon an evil life than by older offenders'. (p.89) The supervision of dance halls, however difficult it was, 'proved to be work for which educated policewomen are particularly well fitted'. (p.85) Education was particularly useful to the policewoman, who was able to reassure the public by being able to distinguish the planet Venus from a dropping bomb. (p.88) There seems to be a distinction here between 'education' and 'knowledge'. Certainly Mary was able to use the latter to her own advantage with respect to the Defence of the Realm Act (DORA): 'The only advantage of "DORA" was that certain sections could be quoted to strengthen any argument, and in the general ignorance no one ventured to question either their accuracy or their application.' (p.91) This is an astonishingly revealing statement. Mary wanted power at any price.

The provision of policewomen for the Ministry of Munitions led to the formation of training schools run jointly by the WPS and the woman patrols, in Bristol, Liverpool and London. Over 1,000 women, trained by the WPS, were at work up and down the country. Mary and Margaret Damer Dawson were invested by the king with the Order of the British Empire on 13 February 1918 at Buckingham Palace. Public acceptance and the royal seal of approval suggested a bright future for this redoubtable force of women.

Mary and Margaret Damer Dawson believed firmly that their work would continue after the war, once their unique contribution to the welfare of women and children was recognised. They had ambitious plans for the WPS.

Both women were extremely fond of children and this, along with their growing concern with women in danger of exploitation by men, prompted Margaret to:

> open a separate set of books to deal with the detail of certain cases, so that with a quick survey the salient facts could easily be got at … The women police were human first, and policewomen only in the second place; and many of them felt that they simply *had* to render help to their unfortunate fellow-creatures when there seemed to be no other way to rescue them from threatening disaster.[30]

A Benevolent Fund was created, financed by public donations, subscriptions from WPS members, and some police forces. The fund was administered by Inspector Champneys, who devoted her later life to the welfare of children and single parents. She gave evidence to the Select Committee appointed to examine the principle and practice of child adoption, which reported in 1920; and served on the executive committee of the National Council for One-Parent Families from 1925 to 1928.

The WPS carried out their work with enthusiasm. 'During six months, in 1917, no less than five hundred women were picked up on street patrol and given immediate assistance.'[31] This assistance included 'admonition', and may well have been less popular with the rescued than with other organisations, including the Salvation Army, the YWCA, and the Church Army

Training Homes who, according to Mary, expressed their encouragement and support. 'Whenever possible such agencies were called upon, but it soon became evident that an organisation directly under the Women Police Service would be a great advantage, so that their own methods of discipline and training and their own influence might be uninterrupted.'[32] This link between 'assistance' and 'admonition' is chilling. Mary is enjoying exerting power, exercising her will over those less fortunate than herself.

The Benevolent Department seems to have attracted sufficient funds to enable it to set up a baby home at The Elms, Aldington, Kent in 1917 (later moved to Hythe, also in Kent, and renamed the Damer Dawson Memorial Home for Babies, in honour of Margaret Damer Dawson, after her death). A short piece of silent film exists with the legend, 'In memory of their founder and first Commandant the Women Police have instituted a sea-side Home for poor mothers and babies'. There are shots of mothers and their babies standing outside the home in Hythe (a substantial house), and policewomen with nurses and babies inside. Another shot shows a police-woman in uniform on a train (wrongly described in the caption as a man), holding a baby out of the window for a woman to kiss. Mary is standing on the platform. She is also pictured at the home, holding a baby wrapped in a luxurious shawl and watching a baby being bathed. Throughout the film, she looks confident and happy, smiling broadly at the camera.[33]

7

A Rude Disillusionment

We had always meant our Service to go on after the war; we had supposed somehow that, when the Germans were beaten, our activities with the khaki armies would cease, and we should be drafted straight into civil police routine … We planned great things for the peace-time organisation of policewomen all over the country. But almost immediately we received a rude disillusionment.[1]

Mary may be forgiven for assuming that women would continue to work in policing after the war, and that the WPS would automatically form the foundation of a female force, led by the women who had served their country in army towns and munitions factories: work for which they had been thanked, honoured and praised. There were inevitably problems of disorder attached to large-scale demobilisation and troop movements. Mary claims that white slavery and the sale of drugs was rife in London, and that the work of the Women Police Service was increased rather than diminished by the end of the war. But the authorities had other ideas about civilian policing: 'We were given official thanks for all we had done to help England in the war, and told to disband as quickly as we could.'[2]

Mary was bitterly disappointed. She had an interview with the Police Commissioner, Sir Nevil Macready, in which she tried to persuade him that the WPS still had a role to play; but Sir Nevil was adamant that women police would 'pinprick the men'.[3] This is what he told Mary; in fact, he was already making plans for his own female force. The *Daily Mail* reported on 3 October 1918 that, 'a force of women police is to be created for London, officially recognised, under the control of the Commissioner of Metropolitan Police, and subject to the same discipline as the men'.[4] In an interview with the *Daily Mail*'s reporter, published the next day, he went on to say that women without any voluntary experience might be preferable, as he 'had a great objection to the amateur in any form'.[5] Mary was puzzled by this apparent contradiction: Macready wanted women with no experience, but he didn't want amateurs. She didn't see her own force of women as being in any way amateur. On the contrary, they were trained, disciplined women. But they were controlled *by women*. Macready wanted a return to the pre-war status quo, with men firmly in charge.

Single women were surplus to requirements after the war. There were now too many of them (war deaths and an influenza epidemic had killed thousands of the men some of them might have married), and too many had acquired skills which had previously been exclusive to men. This perceived problem was solved to some extent by shipping them overseas, to Canada, Australia and New Zealand. But many, like Mary, stood their ground and refused to go away.

Macready's Metropolitan Women Police Patrols (MWPP) did, in fact, recruit some ex-WPS members. The area of operation of his force was, in any case, confined to the Metropolitan area. County constabularies were still requesting policewomen from the WPS, and Mary claims in *Lady in Blue* that, 'we had somewhere over a thousand trained and experienced women, freed from their special war police duties, and a good many of them were looking forward to permanent jobs as peace-time policewomen'. (p.49) Nonetheless, the WPS was forced to cut down its organisation to a minimum: funds were low, and there were not enough jobs for the trained women on their books.

There were still those who approved of the WPS. In July 1919, a royal garden party was held at Buckingham Palace for representatives of the women's war services. Mary spoke to the Prince of Wales who, she says in *Lady in Blue*, 'asked several questions about the Women Police, and was emphatic in his praise of our four years' service'. (p.47) Far more important, though, was the recognition of Sir Leonard Dunning, Inspector of Constabulary, who was reported as saying that 'a number of municipal and county authorities were wise enough to see that there was work for women in a police force. He for a great many years had believed in them and had encouraged the police authorities to adopt women as part of the regular police.'[6]

These remarks were made at a celebration hosted by the WPS of their 'permanency in civilian life' at the Hyde Park Hotel, attended by a number of chief constables, as well as the WPS supporters. *The Times* reporter praises:

> the neat dark blue uniform of the policewomen, their close-cropped heads, and their kindly yet shrewd expressions [which] make them a very businesslike and attractive looking body … Commandant Damer

Dawson was greeted with 'For he's a jolly good fellow' when she rose to speak. The 'he' was not altered to 'she' because in the women police senior officials are all addressed as 'Sir'.

In thanking those present for their gifts, Margaret Damer Dawson remarked on the cohesion of the WPS. 'She said they had worked together for five years and three months without a quarrel or a split in their forces, and she hoped that the same spirit would prevail in future.'[7] There had, of course, been major disagreements in the early days which led to the demise of Nina Boyle, but these were now forgotten. Worse was to come: not from within, but from the new enemy – the Metropolitan Police.

The year 1920 was Mary Allen's *annus horribilis*. In February, Sir William Horwood, the Assistant Commissioner of the Metropolitan Police, put his foot down. He wrote to the WPS, telling them that their uniform 'closely resembled' that of the Metropolitan Women Police Patrols (MWPP), and that they must stop wearing it: 'In his letter the Commissioner pointed out forcibly [*sic*] that we were rendering ourselves liable to fines of £10 apiece by "masquerading" in a uniform that could be mistaken for that of his own Patrols, and that we were absolutely "unofficial and unauthorised".'[8] The injustice of the charge of masquerading was not only untrue; it was grossly unfair to the women – Margaret Damer Dawson and Mary Allen – who had designed the uniform in 1914 and worn it throughout the war, during which time they were serving the best interests of the civilian population, with the sanction of chief constables and government.

A Home Office inquiry was set up in February 1920, under the chairmanship of Major Sir John Baird MP. The purpose of the committee on the Employment of Women on Police Duties, known as the Baird Committee, was to examine the question of equality between men and women in the police service. The Metropolitan Women Police Patrols had been operating for several months, and it was this organisation with which the committee was concerned. However, the committee was unable to ignore the fact that WPS officers were still working for chief constables outside London.

The Metropolitan Police Commissioner at the time was still Sir Nevil Macready, although he was to resign two months later. (He was succeeded by the Assistant Commissioner, Sir William Horwood, a man of greater mettle than Sir Nevil.) Macready wrote to the Home Secretary, expressing the hope that, 'Miss Damer Dawson or any of her other satellites will not be included [on the Baird Committee]'.[9] They were not, although they were called as witnesses.

Macready told the committee that he had overlooked the WPS when putting together his own force of women police because its leaders were mostly former militant suffragettes. (He later wrote a letter to the Bridgeman Committee in 1924, in which he stated that 'the main point was to eliminate any women of extreme views – the vinegary spinster or blighted middle-aged fanatic'.)

Further evidence of Macready's distaste for the WPS leaders was evident in the way he raised the case of the 'Drunk Man'. A couple in Edinburgh whose son had gone missing saw a photograph in a newspaper of a man being arrested by two policewomen and put into their motorcycle sidecar. The parents wrote to the Metropolitan Police and asked them to find out if that man was their missing son. Macready declared in his evidence that this request showed how women masquerading as legitimate officers were confusing the public by issuing such photographs, which were in any case fakes. The drunk man was, according to Macready, in fact a woman dressed as a man.

The photograph of the drunk man was indeed a fake, one of a series of publicity photographs. This one was taken to illustrate Mary's assertion that 'The Commandants would pick up in their side-cars soldiers the worse for liquor, and convey them to safety'.[10] The drunk man is without doubt Superintendent Isobel Goldingham, who apparently was in the habit of dressing in men's clothing. Comparison of Miss Goldingham's photograph in *The Pioneer Policewoman* (facing page 120) with that of the drunk man shows an unmistakable resemblance in face and figure.

Neither Mary Allen nor Margaret Damer Dawson denied this cross-dressing allegation before the committee; but in the WPS 1920–21 Annual Report they claimed that the young man in question was an actor, a 'respected member of a well-known company', who would be willing to testify on oath. A similar photograph of a 'child rescue' appears to have been taken at the same spot in the same street. These are clearly staged shots for the purposes of publicity, intended to show the WPS as a well-equipped force (they had four motorcycles, three of them with sidecars) doing the important work of keeping the public safe from harm on the streets. In fact, their clumsy deception demonstrated a gulf between reality and the myth the WPS wished to create. 'In catching the WPS off guard, Macready revealed the tenuousness of the image-maker's control over the imaging process itself.'[11]

Macready's uniform for the Metropolitan Women Police Patrols was certainly modelled on that of the WPS. However, in asserting that his own force was genuine, and that the WPS was bogus, Macready felt justified in describing the WPS uniform as a parody of the real thing, as worn by the MWPP. He was attacking the WPS on two fronts: firstly, by showing them to be capable of disingenuous deceit; and secondly by attempting to undermine their characters. Although masculine clothing and cropped hair were fashionable in the 1920s, Mary Allen was doing something quite different in her adoption of a military-style uniform (which she wore in public at all times). She was trying (and indeed succeeding) to look like a man. Quite apart from the fact that the WPS was run by women who happened to be lesbians (and Macready hated lesbians), their unsuitability to head a women's police force was, in the eyes of Macready, to take upon themselves the authority which properly belonged to men. The WPS was a force of women run by women; as opposed to the MWPP, which was ultimately controlled by men. Margaret Damer Dawson may have been unwise in her choice of language when she told the Baird Committee, 'We have enough funds to equip a small standing army of policewomen.'

On 18 May 1920, Margaret Damer Dawson died at Danehill, the home she shared in Hythe with Mary. Mary was with her when she died. Margaret was only 46, and the cause of death – valvular heart disease and syncope – is shocking in a woman who had led such a vigorous life. Mary describes her illness as brief and apparently slight, and she declares that it was 'undoubtedly … hastened by her bitter disappointment at the treatment she received after the war'.[12] Typically, Mary says nothing about her own feelings: the words she uses in *The Pioneer Policewoman*, 'shattering blow' and 'deep personal grief' (pp.171–2) are applied generally to all who knew her. But there can be no doubt that Mary suffered greatly at the loss of her friend, colleague and lover.

Margaret Damer Dawson was buried in the churchyard at Lympne in Kent, near Danehill on 22 May, two days after her death. In a very simple ceremony, attended by her mother, Lady Walsingham, members of Margaret's police force dropped sprigs of rosemary into the grave. A memorial was erected in her honour by the WPS: a tall cross in the south-east corner of the churchyard. Mary was the sole beneficiary of her will, but when probate was granted on 23 June 1921, the gross value of Margaret's estate amounted to £355. The net value was nil. Mary continued to own and live at Danehill for many years. It is possible that Margaret, a wealthy woman, had made over a proportion of her assets to Mary before she died. She had undoubtedly used a great deal of her own money to keep the WPS afloat.

'A Correspondent' described Margaret Damer Dawson in *The Times*:

> The most feminine of women, with a gentle voice and quiet manner, she
> yet went further than other uniformed women in adopting the outward
> symbols of male authority. She cut her hair close to her head, a fashion
> in which many of her inspectors followed her, and it was the rule of her
> force that superior officers were addressed as 'sir'. With the outward sym-
> bols, however, the apparent masculinity entirely disappeared. Everything
> that was young found in her a protector.[13]

The author of this eulogy, if not Mary Allen herself, shares Mary's opinion
of Margaret Damer Dawson as a most gentle woman.

A weaker woman than Mary might have thrown in the towel at this
lowest point in her public and personal life. But with typical determination,
she became commandant of the WPS: 'That I should instantly have been
nominated as Chief in Miss Damer Dawson's place was perhaps only a natural consequence of events. In any case, my succession was unquestioned.'[14]

Mary's first decision as Chief was to ignore the commissioner's order to
disband her force. Acknowledging that the WPS had effectively lost London
to the MWPP, she concentrated her efforts on work outside the metropolis,
fulfilling in person all Margaret's outstanding engagements. Mary claimed
disingenuously in *The Pioneer Policewoman* that she had no previous experience of public speaking, and had to 'rely on my own fervour of interest and
my wide knowledge of the subject to carry me through'. (p.173) This was
certainly not the case. She had addressed numerous meetings as a suffragette,
sharing platforms with the WSPU leaders on many occasions.

Only one month after Margaret Damer Dawson's death, Mary went to
Scotland to speak to chief constables, and she opened the WPS Scottish
Headquarters and Training School at St Andrew's Square in Edinburgh:
a short-lived venture through insufficient funds. She was keen to train
women in Scotland to take on the dual function of policewoman and
probation officer: a role her own sister, Dolly (Mrs Hampton), had filled
so successfully in Richmond, that the Metropolitan Police had paid her a
wage of 30s a week. Mary praises the preliminary work done in Scotland
by Inspector More Nisbett, who she describes as one of the WPS's ablest
speakers.[15] Iveigh More Nisbett was, like Mary, a former suffragette who
eventually followed the same regrettable political path as Mary herself.

On 7 March 1921, Sir William Horwood, now Commissioner of the Metropolitan Police, applied at Westminster Police Court for summonses:

> against various members of what he termed 'a social organization known as the Women Police Service' of 109 Victoria-street, Westminster. The summonses, addressed to the commandant, the superintendent, a chief inspector, an inspector and a sergeant, set out that, not being members of the Metropolitan Police Women's Patrol, they, without permission of one of his Majesty's Principal Secretaries of State, wore uniforms having the appearance and bearing distinctive marks of the uniform of the Metropolitan Police.[16]

The hearing was fixed for the afternoon of Wednesday, 16 March, and it was stated that the commissioner would give evidence in person.

The defendants appeared in their uniforms, led by Mary as Commandant. Alongside Mary were Superintendent Isobel Goldingham, Chief Inspector Edith Champneys, Inspector Mary M. Barnett and Sergeant Winifred Nora Sims. They all pleaded not guilty. Mr Muskett, for the prosecution, described the WPS as 'an organization of social workers holding no official standing whatever' which, although useful during the war, 'had persistently and obstinately continued to wear the uniform, notwithstanding the efforts of successive Commissioners of Police. Their uniform was on similar lines to that of the Women's Patrol of the Metropolitan Police Force, and this constituted a grave inconvenience.' In his evidence, Sir William Horwood referred to 'many complaints'; but he added that 'he did not desire to suppress the activities of the Women Police Service'. In cross-examination, Sir William made the extraordinary claim that he had no knowledge of the WPS work for police forces in thirty boroughs, nor of their work in Ireland. 'If this is so,' said the defence, 'do you still say they are not entitled to wear the police uniform?' Sir William's reply was: 'Not in the Metropolitan Police area.'[17]

There can be no doubt from this exchange that the WPS was only being prosecuted because they were causing offence to the Metropolitan Police. Indeed, in his continuing evidence on 21 March 1921, Sir William stated that, 'if there was a modification [to the WPS uniform] so as to leave no confusion, he would be satisfied'.[18] In fact, he would never be satisfied unless the WPS – and Mary Allen – disappeared altogether.

The outcome of the hearing was that the magistrate decided to treat the case as one for a magisterial decision only, and not a punishment of the defendants. The five representatives of the Women Police Service were each fined 10*s*, with Mary ordered to pay 10 guineas costs. In a report in *The Times* of 5 May 1921 it was stated that the matter of the uniform changes demanded by Sir William Horwood had been referred to the Home Secretary, who had decided not to become involved. 'Mr Kingsbury, for the defence, said he submitted certain proposals made by his clients for the consideration of the Home Office, but now the door was slammed in their faces.'

The WPS agreed to change its name to the Women's Auxiliary Service (WAS), and to modify their uniform. Mary was quick to announce the changes she proposed in *The Times*:

> The uniform will still be blue, and in outline and cut will not be changed. Certain details, effected by the introduction of red, will, however, mark the general appearance of the members of the service and make them distinctive. The naval cap will be piped with red, and the badge in blue enamel and silver will bear the present motto of the Service, signifying 'First in the Field', on a red scroll. The buttons will be black with the letters WAS on them. Red epaulets will be worn on which the rank of the wearer will be marked in black braid.[19]

It is hard to believe that the details of these changes were sanctioned by anyone but Mary herself: they still left considerable room for confusion; and there was still no absolute ban on the WPS, now the WAS, working on the streets of London.

Mary summarises the facts of this case briefly in *The Pioneer Policewoman*:

> The Service had been officially recognised during the war as the agents of the Government for the supply of policewomen for HM munitions factories. The summonses were issued at the very time when the Service was supplying trained women to the police authorities in Ireland, there being no other organisation competent to undertake this task. It was an extraordinary situation. (p.177)

She believed that the prestige of the Women Police Service, henceforth the Women's Auxiliary Service, was increased rather than diminished by the case. This may have been true; but the WAS was in financial difficulties and, because the policing of London had been a large part of their work, they needed to find jobs elsewhere, which proved difficult.

Mary did her best to promote the WAS, speaking in London and all over the country, and writing to women's organisations, asking them to bring pressure to bear on the authorities, so that the WAS could continue and become stronger. In a letter to the Women's Institute dated 6 May 1921, she asked to be allowed to address the committee, 'in order to place before you certain facts. Your committee would then, after I had explained matters, be able to consider whether they were prepared to take definite action.' Mary's wording is somewhat strange and almost suggests that the WAS are being persecuted. It was certainly the case that some women involved in policing disliked Mary intensely, and were intent on discrediting the WAS.

Mary also addressed the National Union of Societies for Equal Citizenship in August 1922. 'Miss Allen appeared on the platform in a police commandant's uniform, and when she had concluded her address she saluted the assembly in a military fashion.'[20] She made an allegation about the way policemen dealt with female prisoners:

> Opportunities of a wrong kind must occur. I have heard from girls where opportunity has occurred and where constables have gone into their cells. Policewomen had been withdrawn and dismissed on the plea of economy, but it is not so much a matter of saving money as it is a sop to people who do not want us.

Not surprisingly, these vague and unsubstantiated allegations were denied by a 'high official' at Scotland Yard, with a detailed account of the safeguards in place.[21] What Mary said may well have been true; but she failed in this instance to make an unarguable case for the retention of her service.

Mary's energies were not confined to police matters. She threw herself into civic life. In March 1921 she tried to gain a seat as an Independent on the London County Council as a representative of the National Union of Women Teachers. She gained only 581 votes, and came bottom of the poll. In November 1922, she stood as a Liberal Parliamentary candidate for the St George's division of Westminster. Mr J.M.M. Erskine had won the seat as an Independent Anti-Waste candidate in a by-election the previous year, and he defended it now as an Independent Conservative, and the local man. Mary's slogan in the campaign was the astoundingly unimaginative 'Mary Allen, who knows where she is'. Her manifesto gave priority to health, education, housing, equal opportunities for men and women, extension of the woman's franchise, and the recognition as an essential public service of women police. She said that 'economy at the expense of education can only be ruinously dear in the end … children must not be made to pay for the war'.[22] According to *The Times*'s reporter, women from all parties were willing to work for Mary. '"Mind you," said one of them to me, "they would not work for *any* woman. There are women candidates I myself wouldn't lift a finger for. But Mary Allen is the right sort for Parliament, irrespective of party".' Mary's ability to charm women and win their loyalty was remarkable.

At the poll, Erskine won 55.9 per cent of the votes, and held the seat. Mary's share of the vote was a mere 6.5 per cent. This was a grave disappointment. It was with some bitterness that she later wrote that, 'with few exceptions those [women] who have been elected to the House of Commons have shown, so far, no uncommon gifts'.[23] She never stood for Parliament again.

8

DEMANDS FROM ABROAD

Throughout this difficult period of private bereavement and public attack, the WAS was sustained by demands from abroad for its services.

In June 1920, only a month after the death of Margaret Damer Dawson, the British Army's Colonel Winter from Dublin Castle, visited Scotland Yard and asked for fifty trained women to work with the Royal Irish Constabulary. Unable – and perhaps equally unwilling – to meet his request, the commissioner referred him to the WPS, who sent an officer (Chief Inspector Campbell), a sergeant and seven constables to Ireland immediately, and several more women shortly afterwards.

Ormande de l'Eppé Winter, known as 'O' and 'the holy terror', was Chief of Combined Intelligence Services for Ireland, and from spring 1920 had started to recruit agents from abroad to help track down IRA operatives and Sinn Féin leaders.*

Mary's contingent of policewomen arrived wearing their uniforms, which alarmed the detachment of Dublin policemen who met them, knowing as they did how unpopular uniforms were in Ireland. They had been told that the policewomen would be dressed as nuns, nurses or matrons, and they detained them until further orders were obtained from Dublin Castle. The outcome was that Chief Inspector Campbell was allowed to keep her uniform, but the constables were obliged to change into plain clothes.

The role of the policewomen was to accompany raiding parties and search women. Mary visited her officers in Ireland, and was proud of their work. She wrote with relish of the war-like conditions in which her officers served: 'We were intensely occupied in drafting fearless policewomen to Ireland, where a large section of the British Army, complete with artillery,

---

* In the 1920s Winter retired from the army, and was briefly a director of the British Fascisti in London, possibly working as an undercover agent for MI5.

tanks, machine guns, barbed wire, bombs and all the impedimenta of war, was finding its hands so full that it needed assistance.'[1]

However, her accounts of actual experiences are all second-hand reports from her officers. Mary did not involve herself at all in policing in Ireland, delegating this dangerous work to Chief Inspector Campbell. But she did describe a visit with considerable pride:

> Everything was 'hush-hush'. I was met in Dublin, when I landed alone, by a big closed car, which whirled me away I knew not where. In fact, I rather wondered if I were being kidnapped by Sinn Feiners, since I had insisted on wearing my uniform, despite some serious warnings.[2]

After a meeting with the Ulster Government in June 1922, Mary was prevailed upon to send a further twenty women to Belfast for duties in Northern Ireland. These postings kept the WAS afloat to a limited extent, but Mary's trained women were still finding it difficult to secure posts in England. The organisation might have folded, but for another call for help from abroad.

In 1923 the British Army of Occupation in the Rhine Provinces, based in Cologne, became aware of the problems associated with thousands of troops, 'with more money in their pockets than they knew what to do with, and plenty of spare time on their hands in which to get into mischief'.[3] The problems were similar in nature to those the WPS had faced in Grantham in 1914.

Margery Corbett Ashby, President of the International Woman Suffrage Alliance, a former suffragette and a friend of Mary's, visited Cologne in November 1922 having heard of incidences of bad behaviour by British troops with local women. Mary recollected in *The Pioneer Policewoman*:

> She saw and heard enough in a few days to cause her to seek some ame-lioration of such a menace of vice and increasing disease. On her return to England she at once drew me into consultation in my official capacity as one of the most experienced women in the social problems of Great Britain. (p.200)

Typically, Mary shows no doubts about either her own abilities or her experience being suitable to tackle this problem. The two women approached the War Office, asking that 'some responsible person' should begin an investigation into what action was needed. The Commander-in-Chief of the Army of Occupation, Sir Alexander Godley, put the onus on Mary: if she could persuade the local German authorities that her women would be useful, then she would have his blessing. But it was Mrs Corbett Ashby, and not Mary, who was authorised to return to Cologne, consult with the British military authorities and the German civil authorities, and report back. On her return, Mrs Corbett Ashby recommended that the WAS should be asked to provide policewomen for Cologne.

On 15 March 1923, the Adjutant-General, Sir R.D. Whigham, invited Mary herself to go to Cologne and submit to him a report of how women police might best be used there. *The Times* of 9 July 1923 reported on what the Cologne newspapers had to say about, 'the forthcoming institution of Women Police in the City ... The English policewomen are educated persons who have earned the gratitude of their own countrywomen for the tact and humanity with which they have everywhere carried out their duties.'

Mary's description of her first visit to Cologne is unconsciously funny. She seems to have had no understanding of how others saw her; the open-mouthed stares she attracted were, in her mind, expressions of awed admiration. She had travelled in Europe by train as a young woman; and her first visit to Cologne in 1923 was also made by rail. However, she had lost the knack of European travel – perhaps because it had always been previously made under the auspices of her father and the Great Western Railway, where she and her sisters were well looked-after. Mary mistakenly left her train too early, and found herself alone on the German border in the middle of the night:

> I had to spend the night at an inn where no one spoke English, and where every single member of the household and apparently most of the inhabitants of the village made an excuse to bring something in to me, before I had been there an hour, in order to get a glimpse of my uniform![4]

Of course, it was not just the uniform that they came to see: Mary herself was by now a phenomenon: easily mistaken for a man in her appearance and manner and, unusually for the times, unselfconsciously adopting the authority of a man. She used this to good effect the following morning when she persuaded a driver who spoke no English to take her to Cologne: a hazardous journey, as the driver was towing a car, which chased them down every hill:

> I eventually arrived at Cologne after travelling more than fifty miles in this odd fashion, to find the British authorities searching the country-side

for me, supposing that I had been kidnapped or had suffered some delay through the ill-will of a fanatical German who had taken a dislike to my English police uniform.[5]

Mary stayed for ten days, inspecting police cells and the women's prison, welfare and reformatory homes, Salvation Army and convent hostels, a maternity home and a farm colony for girls. She was also present at a medical examination of 'controlled women', and accompanied what she calls the German Moral Police on their tour of inspection, taking part in raids on suspected houses. She addressed meetings: a large public meeting at the Town Hall, and 'a meeting of the representative women of all the organised societies'.[6] She urged her audience to have German women trained by WAS officers, who would then carry on when the British withdrew.

Mary reported back to Whigham with the recommendation that six policewomen be sent to Cologne to patrol the streets and to recruit and train 'a small number of well-educated German women' to work with them. She also suggested that a shelter for homeless women be established, with a German woman medical officer in attendance. Mary emphasised the importance of wearing a uniform, 'as the Germans themselves had declared that un-uniformed women would be of little use'[7] – an argument with which, of course, she wholeheartedly agreed.

These recommendations were accepted, and an agreement was signed on 22 June 1923 between the Secretary of State for War and Miss Mary Sophia Allen, for the engagement of one officer and five constables for a period of six months. Under this agreement, Mary was to receive no remuneration or salary, but expenses incurred in connection with visits to Germany at the request of the Secretary of State would be reimbursed. Uniforms would be provided by the Secretary of State, payment for each policewoman would be £3 10s per week, with free accommodation or 10s per week in lieu.

Mary flew to Cologne five days later, accompanying Inspector Harburn. Ellen Harburn, Mary's companion in Grantham and Hull, 'who possessed a fine record of service, and who was an excellent German scholar',[8] was to take charge of Sergeant Halfpenny and Constables Barnwell, Bazeley, Fisher and Morris when they arrived on 2 July.

This may have been Mary's first experience of flying. Captivated by the novelty and excitement of flight, it was not long before she began to take flying lessons. Mary returned to Cologne three months later, and from time to time thereafter.

Margery Corbett Ashby wrote to *The Times* on 24 December 1923, concerned at a report that the women police were to be withdrawn, after only six months. She praised their 'quiet and wonderful work' in a place where 'the vice and drinking were awful ... To the German girls, workless and poverty-stricken, each young soldier was a millionaire.' Mrs Corbett Ashby urged the authorities to keep the WAS in Cologne, and in a letter published by the same newspaper on 2 January 1924, Katharine Tynan Hinkson called the proposed withdrawal 'a calamity beyond words'. Although the original six-month contract was extended in February 1925 'retaining the services of the women police from month to month, as the duration of the Occupation is now so uncertain,'[9] the WAS were withdrawn in August 1925.

Ellen Harburn's role in the success of the WAS operation was crucial. She trained three German women, who were taken on by local authorities, and was able to foster good relations with the burgeoning German women's police force. However, she was on one occasion recalled from Cologne when she complained about the way prostitutes were dealt with by both the British and Germans. According to her relatives, 'she always felt that Mary Allen (whom, while admiring her in some ways, in other ways she considered a silly woman) might have backed her up more.'[10]

Mary claimed that she persuaded the German policewomen to wear uniforms, by taking photographs of them in civvies and comparing them with similar photographs of the smart British uniformed women. Her assertion that 'I overcame their objections by appealing to an essentially feminine quality'[11] speaks volumes about Mary's conception of what constitutes femininity.

Mary predicted that what she called 'the experiment in Cologne' would have far-reaching results in women's policing, both in Germany and further afield. She already had visions of a world-wide force of women in uniform, trained to her own standards.

Mary was no stranger to foreign travel; thanks to her father's position in the Great Western Railway, she and her sisters had visited European countries when they were young women, travelling in some style, and well looked-after by railway officials. But her experiences of flying woke in her a desire for air travel, and the hope of becoming a pilot herself.

Mary's first major foray abroad under her own auspices was to the United States where, she felt sure, she could help with the development of a women's police force along similar lines to the WPS. She had, in 1918, entertained 'a dozen or more editors of some of the largest American newspapers' at WPS headquarters in November 1918, each one of whom:

was permitted to accompany a policewoman on her beat for one night's survey of London life in the streets … In the same year the Deputy Police Commissioner of New York asked the Women Police Service kindly to supply a uniform and full equipment, which he was able to take back to New York with him.[12]

In 1924, following the success of the Cologne experiment, Mary accepted an invitation from the American National League of Women Voters (founded by Carrie Chapman Catt in 1920, with the aim of helping newly enfranchised women to use their votes responsibly), to give an address to their fifth annual convention in Buffalo, New York. She travelled first class at her own expense, and arrived in New York aboard the *President Harding* on 20 April 1924. A photograph taken on deck shows a Mary more masculine than ever, posed leaning against the rail in full uniform, monocle in eye. The press were delighted:

Cameramen and news-reel operators mobbed me as I walked down the gangway from the ship. Amid an extraordinary babel, they shouted questions at me, waiting for no answers; they flashed innumerable camera-lenses in my face. Within a few hours, I was 'on the films,' and newspaper placards at every corner bore such startling legends as 'ENGLISHWOMAN POLICE CHIEF IN UNIFORM,' and 'MONOCLED LADY COP IN NEW YORK.' The cameramen simply would not release me from their attentions till I had agreed to try controlling American traffic … What intrigued them most of all was my eyeglass. They were quite convinced – and so was the whole of America within twenty-four hours – that it was a sign of office, like the crozier or the Black Rod![13]

Mary is obsessed with the idea that her uniform is a focus for admiration and wonder. There is no hint that she understands that her appearance provoked amusement, at least from the press and some of the bemused onlookers. The *New York Times* was kinder:

Commandant Allen wears the uniform which she and Miss Dawson designed. It consists of a visored cap, tailored shirt with high collar and a four-in-hand, breeches, long-skirted coat, leather belt and high leather boots which reach the hem of the coat. It is of dark blue and a good looking outfit. Women like it: she is proud of the design, and as one talks with her, the feeling grows that she is as truly feminine in all essentials of character and thought as if she busied herself only with pouring tea and household matters.[14]

The women who had invited Mary to America received her kindly and with enthusiasm, particularly Mrs Mary Hamilton, director of New York's recently established Women's Police Bureau, who acted as Mary's 'guide and helper'.[15] Mary was made to feel very welcome by a number of women, including Dr Valerie Parker and Miss Chloe Owings of the American Social Hygiene Association, and Mrs (Florence) Caspar Whitney, a leading New York socialite and director of the National League of Women Voters, as well as by Chief Commissioner Richard Enright of the New York Police, a campaigner for women police who later became a crime writer. 'My welcome was really a wonderful tonic, for I had been overworked before leaving England, and still felt very tired.'[16]

Mary was certainly kept busy on her tour of America and Canada. In Buffalo, she addressed seven luncheons on one day, one after the other, at the same hotel. While her audiences dined, she was offered, between speeches, food she could not eat – lobster and ice-cream – so that she went hungry all day. Some of her audiences were extremely large: nearly 3,000 people heard her address a meeting to celebrate the 64th Convention of the New York Federation of Women's Clubs. At the invitation of Commissioner Enright, she attended a police dinner, accompanied by Mrs Hamilton:

> This was during the Prohibition era, and so I was naturally astonished when Mrs Hamilton told me that we should have to leave about midnight, because there might be some unpleasant episodes and excesses. When the night came, I was surprised to notice uniformed police officers arriving carrying suitcases … as the dinner progressed, the clicking of opened cases ran like the sound of a volley of toy pistols round the table, and bottles of spirits began to appear in all hands.[17]

Mary watched as, one after the other, police officers fell unconscious. She and Mrs Hamilton left before the New York Anti-Vice Society raided the party in the early hours of the next morning when, according to the newspaper report, 'they had discovered a cabaret in progress … in which negro girls were dancing … indecently'.[18] Mary became aware that police corruption was rife in New York; Richard Enright's resistance to corruption was to lose him his job shortly after Mary's visit. She noticed, too, that illegal drug-use was common, and dealt with admirably by the city's women police.

The differences between American and English policing were of great interest. She remarked, after a visit to the headquarters of the Buffalo women police that its staff 'includes four white policewomen as well as a number of coloured women. In some cities it has been considered advisable to appoint a certain number of coloured policewomen, just as during the last year or two there have been coloured men added to the police forces.'[19] Mary's superior attitude to black women, although perhaps typical of the time she lived in, is still repugnant to the modern reader: 'The black girl officials looked typically good-natured and eager, and I was forcibly reminded by them of H.G. Wells' prophecy, in his novel *When the Sleeper Wakes*, of a whole world policed by coloured people, since they certainly make an excellent type of police officer.'[20]

Mary has little to say about Canada, except that their policewomen did not wear uniform, which she thought was a mistake. A report of her visit to Toronto in the *Toronto Daily Star* concentrates on her appearance:

Her cap is dark blue trimmed with a line of silver on the front with the badge of the women police. She wore a dark blue coat, whose lining being red shows up to great advantage and is reminiscent of some officer's uniform under the Empire regime.

'I designed the uniform myself,' said Commandant Allen to The Star. 'When Miss Damer Dawson and I started police work in England, we submitted the uniform to the authorities who accepted it.'

Commandant Allen wears her hair short. It is not bobbed, the back of her head is cropped short like a man's. 'I am so much freer and easier like that,' she explained. 'No, I do not advocate short hair for all women, but in my work it is necessary.'

'Why do you wear a monocle?' she was asked.

'It is so essentially English,' Commandant Allen answered, 'and besides I have one eye weak, so it is necessary for me. When I read, I use glasses.'[21]

In giving her opinion of the Sunday laws in Canada, she told *The Star*'s reporter:

Personally I do not agree with the idea of no games on Sundays. I think the more amusements there are on Sunday, the less likely young people will be of getting into trouble. Nothing leads so much to the police courts than an idle day. As far as the question of prohibition is concerned, it is too early for me to make any statement, although from what I have seen in the United States most people seem to be against it. You may feel sure, however, that I shall not violate the liquor laws while I am in Canada.

A film clip of Mary in Canada shows her smiling and apparently happy, posing on the street beside a No Parking sign, her hair severely razor-short beneath her peaked cap.[22]

Mary visited New York three times during her tour, which also included Detroit, Chicago, Paterson NJ and Toronto in Canada. In Detroit, she found what she considered the best women police system in the world, under the leadership of Commissioner Eleanor Hutzel, a pioneer in drug rehabilitation, and author of a police manual for women. In Detroit, she observed with approval, women were only ever arrested by policewomen.

In Chicago, Mary found that more than forty policewomen were employed 'of a rather more uncompromising type than I had met elsewhere in the United States,' which she thought inevitable, given the role women played in the Chicago gangs which, she was shocked to discover, 'were allowed to perambulate the city openly in armoured cars'.[23] She attended a trial which was openly rigged; and met a female gangster who held court in prison: 'The crowd [outside the prison], noticing my now famous uniform, seriously supposed that I had journeyed from England specially to see their latest criminal sensation, and they continuously cheered my progress.'[24]

Mary also sat in on the Domestic Relations Courts in Chicago, which, she asserts, helped young people drifting apart 'to start afresh and give love another chance'.[25]

Among the notable people Mary met in America was the millionairess Mrs Mina Van Winkle, who was head of the Washington Women Police, a department which she had instigated herself, and President of the International Association of Policewomen. 'She and I came in for a certain amount of comment on the occasion of a big dinner we attended, she wearing a white satin evening dress and pearls, and I in uniform.'[26] Again, Mary shows her obsession with uniforms. She claims that the lack of uniforms for women police in America led people to believe that there were no policewomen at all in that country. Her mission to America seems, according to her own account, to have been entirely one of promoting the wearing of the all-important uniform:

Both in Canada and in the United States, to wear or not to wear uniform is one of the burning questions continuously argued, and apparently, to judge by its effect, my own simple but well-cut uniform was considered the most forcible [*sic*] argument in favour of its adoption, especially when I had emphasised its undoubted force as a deterrent to misdemeanour and immorality.[27]

In June 1925, Mary was invited to attend the International Police Exhibition and Congress at Karlsruhe in Germany. This two-week exhibition was largely devoted to the promotion of new police technologies, and Mary sent an exhibit of WAS uniforms, photographs and literature for display. She travelled by air, with Inspector Tagart, stopping off on the way in Zurich, where she addressed a meeting of women interested in the question of women police, there being none apart from a woman sub-inspector in the Police Welfare Department 'who does not wear uniform'.[28] Mary rounded off her trip with visits to Basle and Vienna, where the chief police officer, Dr Schober, later Chancellor of Austria, invited her to attend a similar conference in Berlin the following year. She was met at the airport in Karlsruhe by Dr Lothar Barck, author of *Ziele und Aufgaben der weiblichen Polizei in Deutschland* (Aims and Responsibilities of Women Police in Germany, 1928). Her visit brought home to Mary the advantages of policing an island, which 'makes the entry of foreign criminals a matter of great difficulty'.[29]

Mary travelled to Paris in June 1926 to the International Committee for Women Police, established at the Tenth Congress of the International Women Suffrage Alliance. She addressed a large and appreciative international audience on the subject of women police, and the congress formed a resolution asking for all the things Mary herself had been agitating for, including women having the same status and powers as their male colleagues, and the right to wear uniform.

At the 1926 International Police Congress and Exhibition, where she was the only policewoman present, Mary was able to address an audience of delegates from more than forty countries, calling upon all governments to consider the question of appointing women police. Her resolution was passed unanimously, which Mary regarded as one of the greatest triumphs of her career. She believed that it was the stimulus for the formation of Women Police Services throughout the world. These European conferences were opportunities for what we call networking today, and Mary heard much that shaped her political views.

Helen Bourn Tagart, a prominent WAS member, had become Mary's constant companion in every enterprise, accompanying her on tours, and always standing behind her in photographs. Born in Bath in 1876, she was just over a year older than Mary. She was the granddaughter of a wealthy American, and came from a close-knit family. She kept in touch with her sister and two brothers throughout her life, but in 1929 she made a will leaving everything to Mary: an indication of the importance of Mary in her life. In this year, Mary and Helen were photographed together in Berlin. Their appearance is such that they could easily be mistaken for men. Although they are dressed in identical uniform coats and caps, it is noticeable that Helen's overcoat is buttoned like a man's (with the buttons on the right-hand side).

When she returned from her 1924 American tour, Mary learned to fly at the Stag Lane aerodrome in Hendon. Mary and Helen joined the London Flying Club which was based at Hendon. Among their fellow pupils were Lady Bailey and Lady Heath; Amy Johnson's name is dropped into Mary's account in *Lady in Blue*, although it is doubtful whether she ever met her: if she had, she would undoubtedly have recorded her conversation with the queen of flight. Sufficient for the purposes of name-dropping is Mary's comment that, 'We did not dream that this purposeful young woman in oily overalls would shortly astound the world by flying her ancient second-hand Moth alone to Australia!'[30] Later, Mary and Helen joined the Cinque Ports Flying Club, where they undertook dual instruction.[31] Mary made her first solo flight in November 1932.[32] There is no record, however, of her ever qualifying for a pilot's licence.

At home, Mary was still fighting the corner of women in public life against male critics of the concept of sex equality. On 10 December 1925, a letter appeared in *The Times* under the signature of A.H. Henderson-Livesey, author of *The Women Police Question*, who declares uniformed women police to be 'useless', and the move for their appointment due to 'manifestly artificial agitation':

> The suggestion that there is any demand from the normal womanhood of the country for the appointment of women police can only be described as preposterous. Feminism is an urban disease: outside of London it has no force and the County police authorities show their robust commonsense by acting according to their belief that the duties of a uniformed police officer can only be properly performed by a man, and a real man – as distinct from a supporter of the feminist movement – at that.

Henderson-Livesey's dislike of feminists, and particularly of women who dress and behave in an unwomanly fashion, is clear. Mary is, as usual, quick to reply. Her response is published the following day, 11 December, asking to be allowed to 'say a word on behalf of the Women Police, upon whom Mr Henderson-Livesey has to-day exercised his caustic pen'. She points out that support for the appointment of additional women police comes from 'many local authorities, and the representative women's organizations of all parties' as well as the 'normal' women, who had recently petitioned the Home Secretary for his support; although her claim that 'the movement since 1914 has gained the support of the Commissioner of the Metropolitan area' is somewhat contentious. Mary concludes: 'if the sexes are equal, as to-day surely no one denies, why should men abrogate to themselves the right to deal with women alone?'

Mary has either misunderstood Henderson-Livesey's argument, which is unlikely; or she has deliberately chosen to ignore it. But less than six months later, the General Strike gave her an opportunity to show that women police were a force to be reckoned with, which could be called upon in an emergency.

9

A GOOD DEAL OF FEMININE SPITE

In 1926 the looming General Strike provoked a typically indignant response in Mary, who saw subversive forces everywhere:

> Trades Unions, from performing vital and praiseworthy offices for Britain's workers, had changed after the war into domineering political organisations whose chief object seemed to be to grasp the government of the country.
>
> May 1st, 1926, being International Labour Day, was chosen by them as an appropriate occasion on which to put a pistol to the head of England, and demand her surrender to a Communist coup.[1]

Mary was unmoved by the plight of coal miners facing wage reductions, deteriorating working conditions and longer hours. Fear of Communism was widespread, and her xenophobia triumphed over her humanity.

Having exhausted all possibilities of employment by the government after the withdrawal of her women from Cologne, Mary saw the General Strike as an ideal opportunity to promote the potential of the Women's Auxiliary Service (WAS) as a sizeable trained force of women ready to help undermine the strike, and to show the authorities how wrong they had been in spurning her organisation.

She went into action immediately, calling for volunteers for the WAS Emergency Corps in a BBC radio appeal. The response was gratifying: over 2,000 women came forward: 'Two aeroplanes, nearly two hundred cars, hospitality, sleeping accommodation, and several complete houses were put at our disposal.' To Mary's joy, Emmeline Pankhurst came out of retirement to help: 'Fearlessly, this grand woman travelled and addressed sullen gatherings, doing the work of two ordinary people, and soothing down some of the bitterest elements in our population.'[2] The prime minister's wife, Lucy

Baldwin, joined forces with Mary, and Viscountess Rhondda offered the use of her offices in Victoria Street for the Emergency Corps' transport section. Seven separate branches were set up in London to deal with the demand for cars for women workers, and recreation and rest rooms for working women were opened.[3]

Mary's enthusiasm for the work of strike-breaking ('my offices buzzed night and day like an overturned beehive'[4]) is typical of her lust for organising and getting noticed – and for danger: her drivers and their cars were frequently attacked. The nine-day strike offered a short-lived period of glory; but Mary was ready for any further outbreaks. 'Many of those who had proved so valuable as volunteers offered to remain on an emergency roll in case of future national need, and thus formed the nucleus of a powerful organisation for combating [*sic*] any further attempt at national sabotage.'[5] She relished the opportunity to serve her country, and to be recognised for that service. Tellingly, her expression of satisfaction at a job well done is couched in military terms:

> It is an axiom that nothing saps the energy of an army so much as a long spell of peace, and some years had passed now since most of us had had actual first-hand experience in uniform, in tasks that were of direct assistance to the Government, and at its request.[6]

The virulence of Mary's hatred of foreigners and Communists (which were more or less synonymous to her mind) is extraordinary. She loathed with a passion any threat to the maintenance of the divisions in society. She was a conservative in every sense of the word.

Despite all her hard work during the General Strike, the Women's Auxiliary Service continued to be a thorn in the flesh of the establishment, and particularly when they operated within the London Metropolitan area. A Home Office dossier on the activities of Mary Allen was opened in July 1927 as a result of a letter from the Metropolitan Police Commissioner (Mary's old adversary, Sir William Horwood), to the Secretary of State at the Home Office, Sir William Joynson-Hicks. This letter concerned a complaint made about Mary Allen by a Miss A. Freemantle, and suggested that the Secretary of State should 'call on Miss Allen for an explanation of her conduct'.[7]

Miss Freemantle of 9 Nevern Square, Earls Court, had written to the commissioner, complaining that 'Commandant Allen, of the Women's Police' had been making enquiries about her. She asked by what authority Mary acted for the police. A chief inspector and a sergeant interviewed Miss Freemantle, who said that a rumour had sprung up that she had performed

1. The Allen family (*c.* 1907). (*Standing left to right*) Janet, Mary, Thomas Isaac; (*seated left to right*) Denys, Christine, Margaret Sophia. (Author's collection)

2. Mary as a suffragette, wearing her hunger strike medal. (Author's collection)

3. Self-Denial Week, Bristol 1910. (*Left to right*) Edith West, Mary Allen, Miss Staniland, Elsie Howey, Mrs Dove-Willcox. (Museum of London)

4. Margaret Damer Dawson (*left*) and Mary, 1915. (Author's collection)

5. Mary (*centre*) with four members of her force, 1916. (National Portrait Gallery)

6. 'The Drunk Man'. Mary driving the motorbike, Margaret behind, Isobel Goldingham in the sidecar. (Getty Images)

7. Isobel Goldingham. (Author's collection)

8. Arriving at New York onboard the SS *Harding*, 30 April 1924. (Getty Images)

9. With Inspector Tagart in Berlin, 18 June 1929. (Science and Society Picture Library)

10. Members of the Women's Auxiliary Service leaving Victoria railway station, London, to take up duties in Egypt. Mrs Tindal (*left*) and Miss Barnwell, with Commandant Mary Allen (*centre*), 2 January 1930. (Topfoto)

11. The Pyramids, 1930. Helen Tagart and Mary in uniform. Mary has the larger camel. (Author's collection)

12. Commandant Mary Allen of the Women's Auxiliary Service inspecting recruits to the Women's Reserve, Tothill Street, Westminster, London, 29 November 1933. (Topfoto)

13. Members of the Women's Reserve at Reading Aerodrome, January 1934. Mrs E. Battye, Mary's 'personal pilot' (*left*); Mary (*centre*); and two recruits. (Author's collection)

14. Mary in her sixties. Still in uniform. (Author's collection)

15. British Fascist leader Oswald Mosley (*far right*) at a meeting with (*left to right*) Edward J. Hamm, Commandant Mary Allen, A. Raven Thompson, Victor Burgess, A. Gamman and T. Morran, 12 February 1948. (Author's collection)

16. Champion Chu Fuan of Sherhill. (Author's collection)

an illegal abortion. She kept a boarding house, and her lodgers came to her through an agency, and she heard from a gentleman connected with that agency that Mary had called on their secretary, Mr Wimble, and questioned him about Miss Freemantle.

Miss Freemantle wrote to Mary for an explanation. Mary replied at first that she had made a mistake; then denied having made any enquiries at all. Mr Wimble, in his statement to the police, said that he believed Mary to be a police official; he was 'impressed by the demeanour of Commandant Allen and at once thought she was an official connected with the women's police, although she did not say so'. He alleged that Mary said of Miss Freemantle, 'I have a dossier about her'.[8]

The commissioner, who had been waiting to catch Mary out since she appeared at Westminster Court in 1921 charged with impersonating a Metropolitan police officer, consulted solicitors Messrs Wontner and Son, to see if a conviction could be secured against her under Section 10 of the Police Act 1919. Wontners felt that there was insufficient evidence, and suggested that a constable should accost her in the street to ask her 'whether she was a police official and why she was wearing a uniform like the police uniform'.[9] Commissioner Horwood chose to disagree with Wontners' opinion; and he considered the curtailing of Mary's activities to be essential. Wontners had shown that Miss Freemantle was not as innocent as she appeared (although this was immaterial to the question of impersonation); and the Home Office thought that:

> the Commissioner ought to show a much stronger case before inviting the Secretary of State's intervention. His attitude towards her is displayed in the rather ill-judged minute ... in connection with her appearance at the Berlin Police Congress last year. We have no evidence that she does any substantial mischief and certainly there is nothing illegal (as quaintly suggested in [a minute] in the Commissioner's file) or necessarily improper, in her making inquiries 'which none but police officers are entitled to make' or keeping dossiers of people which should not be in the possession of private persons. And the Commissioner's suggestion that the Secretary of State should call upon her for an explanation of her conduct is almost tantamount to inviting the Secretary of State to treat Miss Allen as she is said to have treated Freemantle ... One further point should perhaps be mentioned. It seems to me rather doubtful whether Freemantle's original letter to the Commissioner is really what it purports to be. It is curiously phrased and suggests to my mind that she had previously discussed the matter with someone connected with the police ... The

whole affair seems a little open to the suspicion of having been worked up by someone who had accidentally obtained knowledge of Miss Allen's inquiries; and the identity of Freemantle's mysterious informant might afford a clue.[10]

The Home Office made it clear in a letter to the commissioner dated 16 August 1927 that, in their opinion, a prosecution would not only be ineffective, but would give Mary 'considerable openings for self-advertisement'.[11] This was far from the result Commissioner Horwood hoped for. Wontners' opinion, casting suspicion on the source of Miss Freemantle's complaint, is amply supported by the activities of Mary's enemies. She was undoubtedly a nuisance, and the Metropolitan Police would not let matters rest.

Horwood retired the following year, still smarting over his inability to put a stop to Mary's activities. One of his last acts was to write to *The Times*, stating that, 'Miss Mary Allen has nothing whatever to do with the Women Police of London, who are part of the Metropolitan Police Force'.[12]

In August 1929, the new commissioner, Viscount Byng, forwarded to the Home Office correspondence from Edith Tancred of the Women Police Patrols (WPP) National Committee, asking them to clear up the matter of uniforms.

Edith Tancred, the daughter of a mining and railway engineer and baronet, was one of the founders of the voluntary patrols movement. In 1918 she was appointed Director of the Scottish Training School for Women Police, having first observed the training at the Bristol Training School for Women Patrols and Police, a joint venture between the WAS and WPP which both parties found uncomfortable. Mary claimed that Edith Tancred's WPP copied her own WAS curriculum, which was probably true; but it was a compliment she felt unable to accept.

Miss Tancred insisted that there was confusion at home and abroad about Mary's true role, and she quoted an article in a French publication in which 'Miss Allen is accepted as the head of the Metropolitan policewomen and as wearing their uniform'.[13] The Home Office were of the opinion that 'there is no effective way of getting at Miss Allen except by way of the uniform'[14] but that the WAS uniform was unlikely to be confused with that of the Women Police Patrols. She wrote to *The Times* on 13 March 1931 deploring the Home Office's failure to 'establish the service of women police on a legal basis and ensure that the women members of police forces are properly trained and equipped for the duties they will be called upon to perform'. Miss Tancred was particularly exercised by the fact that the International Council of Women, who had convened in London, and held a 'Pageant of Progress', had 'in ignorance of the non-official character of the Women's Auxiliary Service, invited Miss Mary Allen to send two members of her society to appear in their uniforms as Women Police. The National Council of Women deeply regret and resent this incident.'

The argument between the two women's organisations was now deeply personal. An angry exchange of letters in *The Times* began with Miss Tancred's account of the Home Secretary's dismissal of a request from the National Council of Women for the establishment of a women's police service. Mary wrote a riposte to *The Times* the same day:

> I fear that a letter on the subject of 'Women Police' which appeared in your columns to-day, signed by Miss Edith Tancred, may give a somewhat misleading impression to your readers. I should therefore be most grateful if you would allow me to point out that policewomen in this country have already a 'legal status' which was granted to them in 1916 … We as a country are not backward in regard to the position of policewomen, most of whom are now eligible for pension, granted the power of arrest, and entrusted with important duties.[15]

Mary's icy tone is admirably reproduced in Miss Tancred's swift reply:

> I fear that Miss Allen is not in sufficiently close touch with the movement for women police to realise the dissatisfaction that prevails in every part of the country over the failure of the Home Office to establish women police on a legal basis … The National Council of Women considers that the vital questions of selection and training, qualifications and conditions of service … can only be dealt with by the police authorities themselves.[16]

This is a direct hit at the credentials of Mary's own force, and it was left to another correspondent to defend her position. G. Green-Armytage[17] of 56 Warwick Square, London SW1 writes:

> Miss Tancred's allusion to Miss Allen and her loss of touch with the movement for women police seems to require some explanation. Commandant Allen – to give her the title by which she is known the world over – was, with the late Miss Damer-Dawson, the pioneer policewoman. Together, in the earliest days of the Great War, they founded the Women's Police Service, and it, under its present title of Women's Auxiliary Service, has never ceased its activities or to supply policewomen of a high standard to the provinces and various other organizations. Also, it is through the

inspiration and advice of Commandant Allen that many European countries owe their own force of policewomen today. It is therefore obvious
that Commandant Allen is unlikely not to be fully conversant with all
aspects of this great movement.[18]

Mary couldn't have put it better herself.

The Home Office were not only moved by Edith Tancred's displeasure.
They had their own misgivings about Mary's activities generally. When
Isobel Goldingham proposed in 1929 that Mary should receive a further honour in recognition of her post-war work in Germany (she was
awarded the OBE in 1918 for her work in the munitions factories during
the First World War), it was noted that 'As far as HO is concerned there
is, I take it, nothing doing. Miss Allen's enthusiasm is constantly outrun-
ning her discretion'[19] and 'some of her activities have been rather on the
questionable side'.[20]

The matter of the uniform would not lie down, and in August 1931 the
Home Office reiterated their opinion that 'As regards uniform the position
has been made much more difficult by the adoption of the new Metr. uniform, for, as the WAS newspaper pointed out at the time … the new Metr.
kit is almost a copy of the WAS uniform in 1915. It is obvious that to prosecute Miss Allen for wearing a uniform which (closely) resembles the Metr.
uniform only because the latter was formed from the former wd. expose
the Commr. to ridicule.'[21]

However, having received a despatch from the Foreign Office about
Mary's activities in South America, it was felt that 'we had better warn FO –
in case they should get enquiries from other Representatives abroad – that
she is not all she may appear to be'.[22] This they duly did, stating that:

(a) she holds no official position in this country and her organisation,
the Women's Auxiliary Service (late the Women's Police Service) has no
official standing, and (b) on more than one occasion she has come near
causing embarrassment by representing herself, or allowing herself to be
represented, as holding such a position.[23]

Mary's South American tour had indeed been a great success, and she was
welcomed without question in Brazil and Rio as the leader of the British
women police. She addressed government institutions in Uruguay and
Brazil, and persuaded the President of the Republic of Uruguay to sign a
decree immediately, authorising the employment of women police; and in
Brazil, Sir William Seeds, the British Ambassador, declared:

Contrary to what might have been expected from her uniform and from the rather terrifying press photographs which I have seen of her, Commandant Allen combined a mastery of her craft with a charming, unaffected manner – and an interest in the Brazilian point of view – which won her the genuine liking and respect of the Brazilian ladies. Undoubtedly the star turn of the Congress, she produced a most favourable impression to the Chief of Police.[24]

Meanwhile, Edith Tancred, still on the warpath, wrote in September 1931 to Superintendent Dorothy Peto of the Metropolitan Police complaining that 'our Home Office continues to allow Miss Mary Allen of the Women's Auxiliary Service to pose as a policewoman belonging to the Metropolitan Police Force'.[25] The Home Office responded to the commissioner, who had forwarded Miss Tancred's latest diatribe that, 'the FO would be quite willing to notify all HBM [Her Britannic Majesty's] representatives abroad … On the other hand one hesitates to invoke the assistance of the FO in a matter which (to make no bones about it) does not concern HO very deeply and is mixed up with a good deal of feminine spite.'[26]

IO

WHITE SLAVES

Mary had a keen interest in the purported international trade in women, known as white slavery, which she believed to be intimately connected with narcotics and crime. Her lover and colleague, Margaret Damer Dawson, had been a leading light in the National Vigilance Association, which took over the work of the Belgian Traffic Committee and, through her, Mary became involved in efforts to control this perceived problem.

White slavery became an obsession with Mary, particularly as she saw a role for policewomen in its detection and prevention. She was far from alone: various women's organisations concerned with 'social purity', as well as the women's suffrage movement, churchmen and crusading journalists, expressed fears that large numbers of women were being abducted, bought and sold for sexual purposes.

The 1912 Criminal Law Amendment Act was passed on the basis that such a trade was real and present; and at its conference held in London in July 1913, The International Bureau for the Suppression of the White Slave Trade passed a resolution on the need for the appointment of policewomen in order to control the 'evil trade'.

There were, however, some who disputed the existence of white slavery. In an article published in 1913[1], Teresa Billington-Greig, a suffragette who fell out with the WSPU, and helped to found the rival organisation, the Women's Freedom League, asserted that the 1912 Act had resulted:

> almost entirely by the statement that unwilling, innocent girls were forcibly trapped; that by drugs, by false messages, by feigned sickness, by offers of or requests for help and assistance, girls were spirited away and never heard of again; that these missing girls, often quite young children, were carried off to flats and houses of ill-fame, there outraged and beaten, and finally transported abroad to foreign brothels under the control of large vice syndicates.

This account sums up neatly Mary Allen's own appraisal of the situation. She had no doubt at all that this trade was widespread and a real threat to blameless girls and women. Miss Billington-Greig opposes her, claiming that stories of abductions were exaggerated and often so incredible as to be beyond belief. Moreover, the stories were all 'offered second or third hand' as is the case in all urban myths. She investigated every available reported case most thoroughly, and found no evidence at all to support the argument that white slavery was thriving in Britain. She concludes that:

> these dabblers in debauchery by word of mouth have given us a shocking exhibition of unlicensed slander. That this exhibition has been possible is due in no small measure to the Pankhurst domination. It prepared the soil; it unbalanced judgement; it set women on the rampage against evils they knew nothing of, for remedies they knew nothing about.

This sounds very much like an inter-organisational suffragette tiff, but Miss Billington-Greig's thorough investigation is both admirable and compelling.

At the 1927 League of Nations Conference on the Traffic in Women in Geneva, Mary heard talk of the manufacture and distribution of drugs in what was then called the Near East. Believing that trained policewomen could be helpful in combating this trade, Mary consulted Lord Lloyd on his return as High Commissioner of Egypt and the Sudan. Lloyd had been forced to resign from his post,[2] so her approach was, perhaps, ill-timed; but despite the fact that his view of the value of women police in Egypt was 'not at first so optimistic as I had hoped',[3] Mary states that his advice undoubtedly led to their eventual appointment.

Egypt was under British rule until 1922, when it became independent. But British troops remained in Cairo and the Nile Delta until 1946. In 1951 Egypt demanded that the British withdraw from the Suez Canal zone, and claimed full sovereignty over Anglo-Egyptian Sudan. Egypt was, therefore, still very much British in the 1930s, with most institutions, including the police force, dominated by British military men, who continued to make major decisions on government and policy.

Mary had a passion for travel, particularly by air, and there is no doubt that this passion, along with an overweening self-confidence, prompted her to try and initiate women's police forces all over the world. Europe was not enough and Egypt, an outpost of the Empire, was particularly tempting.

Mary wrote to Ablitt Bey (Walter James Ablitt, Commissioner of the Alexandria Police) who asked her to send him two trained women to attach to his force.[4] Their roles were to include combating the traffic in women,

drug smuggling and the sale of 'indescribable photographs of sexual per-
version' which were allegedly exported from Britain and passed off as
photographs taken in Egypt, with the intention of undermining British
prestige.[5] *Al-Ahram*, a leading Cairo newspaper, made the imminent arrival
of British policewomen front-page news, and conducted a survey of readers'
opinion on the introduction of women into the Egyptian police force. This
survey was launched by the poet Mae Ziyadah, to whom Mary Allen had
sent a letter and a copy of the *Policewoman's Review* asking Mae Ziyadah's
advice about how to proceed. *Al-Ahram* published Mary's article from the
Policewoman's Review, which outlined the benefits to Egyptian society of
women police:

> They could keep an eye on women who had tried to commit suicide.
> They could take statements from women and children in the event of a
> crime and in the event of sexual or other assault they could assist in the
> identification of the assailant, the corroboration of evidence and prepara-
> tion of testimony before the courts. Other duties of policewomen would
> include investigating charges against 'women of ill repute' or charges of
> drunk and disorderly or other immoral conduct levelled against women,
> in which context they could assist in house searches, body searches and
> the surveillance of entertainment halls and furnished flats with female
> tenants. In addition, they could accompany female prisoners from jail to
> the court, conduct searches of female convicts and monitor the condi-
> tions of female prisoners. They could further perform such charitable
> services as locating shelters for homeless women and children.[6]

Prof. Yunan Labib Rizk, the eminent Egyptian historian, comments that,
'One suspects that *Al-Ahram* readers ... would have cast a sceptical eye
over the ostensible benefits. Rarely would they have heard of an Egyptian
woman committing suicide. Odder yet would have been a woman
apprehended for inebriation or other immoral conduct, given that such
behaviour would have cost her reputation and, perhaps, her life',[7] remarks
which indicate how out-of-touch Mary was with the reality of the every-
day lives of women in Egypt.

Only one-third of the 1,026 respondents to Mae Ziyadah's survey
favoured the introduction of women police, and the majority of those were
against foreign women, being already tired of colonial rule. Many of them
pointed out the differences between British concepts of law as it related
to women and those held under Shari'a law. Indeed, some of the newspaper's correspondents were unable to take the matter seriously. 'Most of

the participants in the survey felt that if there were a women's police force its members should be of "incontestable ugliness, scowling countenance and menacing appearance".' One correspondent suggested a police force composed entirely of eunuchs, 'since all the eunuchs that once worked in the country's villas and palaces were now out of work in view of the Westernisation that was taking hold of the country'.

Another account of Mary's proposed introduction of policewomen to Egypt is given by Céza Nabaraoui in the November 1929 issue of the feminist monthly *L'Egyptienne*. Nabaraoui had heard Mary address the 1926 International Police Congress and Exhibition in Berlin. She described Mary as:

> this eminent Chief of Women Police in England ... one of the most popular figures of contemporary feminism. With her commanding appearance and the elegance with which she wears her uniform everywhere, she presented a star-like quality ... she arrived by private plane to deliver her address to the delegates of 45 countries on the benefits of women police. It was reported as a veritable triumph.[8]

As usual, Mary convinces everyone who hears her that she is an official representative of the British police force. Nabaraoui is clearly impressed by Mary: both her appearance and her powers of persuasion. However, Nabaraoui concurs with the opinion of Russell Pasha (Sir Thomas Wentworth Russell), Commandant of the Cairo Police, that 'before beginning to institute women in the police, the Egyptian Government has a much more urgent duty; that is to better the conditions of service of policemen,' and she reports Russell's view that, although he would 'be happy to shake the hand of his charming colleague on her arrival in Cairo, ... however much one might admire the women police of Europe, it is not believed to be possible to create a similar role in Egypt.'

On 2 January 1930 two policewomen bound for Alexandria were photographed leaving Victoria Station in London. Miss Barnwell (a former suffragette imprisoned in 1909 for 'damaging a window in the train by which Mr Asquith returned to London'),[9] and Mrs Tindal. They had undergone rigorous training for their tasks. The two policewomen are dressed in smart belted uniforms with neckties, and carrying white gloves. Standing on the station platform on either side of Mary, they look earnest and apprehensive.

It was not long after the departure of Miss Barnwell and Mrs Tindal that Mary herself visited Egypt, leaving Croydon in February 1930 with Inspector Tagart by air for Marseilles, and continuing to Alexandria by boat.

She was met in Alexandria by Ablitt Bey and other police officials. 'They put a police car at my disposal, gave me *carte blanche* to go where I pleased and see what I chose in the country, and assisted me in every possible way.'[10] On 11 February 1930, Mary arrived in Cairo. She lunched with Sir Percy Loraine, successor to Lord Lloyd as High Commissioner. Sir Percy showed polite interest in the notion of women police in Egypt, but the conversation turned nostalgically to Greece, his previous posting, which Mary intended visiting next. She also met Sir Alexander Keown-Boyd, Director General of the European Department of the Egyptian Ministry of the Interior, 'a keen supporter of the appointment of policewomen'.[11]

In Cairo, Mary met Russell Pasha who, as well as being Commandant of the Cairo Police, was Director of the Egyptian Central Narcotics Intelligence Bureau, formed in 1929. Thanks to Russell's skill and enthusiasm, the bureau hunted down and destroyed many European sources of supply in illegal narcotics and, according to Mary, Russell expressed a particular interest in the work of the two policewomen she had sent out to Alexandria, and asked her to supply two more to assist him in Cairo. Mary inspected the hostel and refuge run by the Cairo branch of the International Bureau for the Suppression of Traffic in Women and Children, and attended a reception in her honour given by the President of the Feminist Union of Egypt, Madam Charaoui Pacha, at which there were many distinguished guests. The February 1930 issue of *L'Egyptienne* reported that:

> During the reception the guests expressed great interest in the two police-women [Mary Allen and Inspector Tagart] and listened with attention to the account of the wonderful work they have accomplished in their own country. We sincerely hope that their colleagues who have just come to Alexandria will soon show in the carrying out of their new duties, what improvement they can make in the purifying of public morals. The whole future of the women police in Egypt will depend on the result of their efforts.

An account of Mary's visit in the *Policewoman's Review* shows that it was not all work:

> Commandant Allen saw the Pyramids of Gizeh, the Sphinx and the desert under ideal conditions, as it was a glorious day with brilliant sun. She was also privileged to see the excavations lately begun under Egyptian direction and some of the discoveries not yet open to the public. The famous Tutankhamen relics in the Cairo Museum proved to be all and more than the accounts of them promised.[12]

A photograph shows Mary and Inspector Tagart seated on camels flanked by Major T.C. Hithersay, officer in charge of the Pyramids Police, and Joseph N. Amal of the Cairo Police, with the Sphinx and a pyramid in the background. Both women are wearing their police uniforms. It is worth considering here how the readers of the *Policewoman's Review*, working policewomen, felt about all this jollification. Mary was above all having fun, and she was unable to keep quiet about it.

The two women chosen by Mary for duties in Cairo were Helen Hoskyn and Barbara de Vitré. Helen Elizabeth Hoskyn was already familiar with Egypt, having been appointed superintendent of the hostel and refuge in Cairo in March 1930, and later appointed as an outside worker. 'Her work in this capacity will bring her into closer touch with the police, and we hope will mean greater co-operation with them.'[13] A teacher of languages, she had retrained as a policewoman in order to concentrate on welfare work.

Barbara de Vitré (who went on to have an illustrious career in the British police service, becoming the first woman assistant inspector) had joined the Women's Auxiliary Service in 1928 and, after six weeks training, moved to the Sheffield Constabulary. On 30 September 1931, she and Hoskyn left London to join the Cairo City Police 'where they were to raise and train a branch of Egyptian policewomen to help eradicate the huge drug-trafficking problem in the Near East'.[14] This date suggests that there was only a short period of special training before they left Victoria Station on 15 October, where they were photographed with Mary, Inspector Tagart and Chief Inspector Campbell. Dressed in mufti, Hoskyn and De Vitré appear less apprehensive than their Alexandrian colleagues.

Mary was delighted with the success of her enterprise:

Both [Hoskyn and De Vitré] have been an unqualified success, and Russell Pasha and others have since expressed entire satisfaction with their work. More policewomen have been appointed in Egypt since, and the first great step has thus been taken towards maintaining order among native women in the outposts of white civilisation.[15]

This last comment reveals Mary's ignorance of, or perhaps indifference to, the growing unrest and resentment of British rule in the colonies. Mary was a staunch believer in the benefits of the Empire to those it ruled.

In Cairo, Mary also visited a women's prison and a hostel 'run by the bureau for the Suppression of Traffic in Women and Children'. Mary is appalled by the trade in women: 'The way they live and the things they are forced to do cannot be described in print; and yet, in spite of such living evidence, there are still people who have never stirred a foot outside England who say that the white slave traffic does not exist.'[16] This was a continuing source of argument between Mary and Teresa Billington-Greig of the Women's Freedom League in the British press and elsewhere.

Mary returned to Egypt at Christmas 1935: 'I found the policewomen I had sent to Cairo and Alexandria still operating with complete success. They had apparently settled down happily with their men colleagues; they had learned Arabic and several native dialects, as well as a number of European languages necessary for work in the ports.'[17] In fact, Barbara de Vitré had resigned from her post in Cairo in April 1932, after only seven months, because of 'the terrible conditions under which she was working (a miserable living situation and poor pay)'.[18]

These visits to Egypt appear to be the last of Mary's foreign adventures. By the end of 1933 she was devoting her energies to domestic politics, and a new role for herself.

II

AN ACCOMPLISHED WRITER

Mary was a prolific writer: of letters, reports, regulations, magazine articles, a magazine for policewomen, and no less than three volumes of autobiography.

In 1925, she published, with the help of Julie Helen Heyneman, *The Pioneer Policewoman*. The book, which gives an account of the Women Police Service since its inception in 1914, was dedicated to the memory of the 'Chief', Margaret Damer Dawson, who had died five years before publication. Mary's use of the royal 'we' in the Foreword seems not to refer to herself and her collaborator, so much as herself alone: 'we owe a great debt of gratitude to our Editor, Miss Heyneman for the patience and good humour with which she has accepted our constant additions, subtractions or emendations to the text.' Julie Helen Heyneman was an artist and writer, born in San Francisco in 1868. She was a friend and pupil of John Singer Sargent, the noted portrait painter.

The Pioneer Policewoman begins with a brief history of policing in England, starting in Anglo-Saxon times and progressing through the Conquest, the reign of Charles II, Bow Street and the Peelers. This overview occupies the first four pages. Mary then pays tribute to the leaders of the suffragette movement for setting aside their aims at the outbreak of war. The First World War seems to Mary to have been a good thing, giving 'immediate birth to aspirations which otherwise would only have gained shape and form slowly after long, hard and bitter travail'. (p.7) Although it is likely that women would have found a place in policing eventually, with or without the intervention of a war, it is probably true that the work of the WPS did much to hasten this innovation, for which Mary receives little credit in official histories of women police.

Mary then moves on to the formation of the WPS and active service during the war. This is the most interesting part of the book. The WPS did sterling work in war-torn towns and cities, and in the munitions factories, and its leaders created a framework for training and organisation which benefited greatly from Mary's own skills in these areas. Her account of the post-war years is mostly taken up with the Home Office enquiry (the Baird Committee of 1920). A whole chapter is dedicated to the death of Margaret Damer Dawson – or rather, to Mary's taking over the WPS after her death – and work in Ireland and Germany, and Mary's visits to the United States and Canada.

Thirty-six pages of *The Pioneer Policewoman* are dedicated to 'The Future', in which Mary outlines her ideas for the role of women in policing. A police woman 'should have clearly defined duties, and should always be considered as an addition to any force, and not as a substitute for a man'. (p.238) Among the services that can be rendered exclusively by women she lists 'inspecting and reporting on the tone of places of amusement,' (p.251) and she is at pains to point out 'the ease with which indecent literature or harmful postcards may be obtained'. (p.255) There is some muddled thinking in Mary's drawing a parallel between the poor standards of food hygiene in England and the evil influence of American movies; but her argument is clear: vice is contagious, and women have a role in eradicating it and creating a better, more moral society.

Mary's preoccupation with vice is evident from 'The Future'. But there is some confusion in her mind about prostitutes, who she sees as at once foolish and evil: 'It was not through the fault of the police alone that the dangerous prostitute was allowed so much liberty to spread infection to coming generations … [a woman] can speak to the giddy girl, before her giddiness makes her slip down the first step towards prostitution and disease.' (p.235)

The Pioneer Policewoman is perhaps most interesting for some of the illustrations: portraits of Mary, Margaret Damer Dawson (looking stern and masculine in her uniform, staring straight at the camera through steel-rimmed spectacles); and Superintendent Goldingham, arms folded and looking to one side. Each portrait shows the image Mary wants to establish of women police. All three women are stern-faced and unsmiling, distinguished by extremely short haircuts and tightly knotted neck ties. Other photographs show the work they do – or wish to suggest to the public that they do: 'Policewomen and children in recreation ground' (facing page 84) shows children with suspiciously tidy hair in a brick courtyard, sitting on the ground holding books and comics; 'Babies at the Damer Dawson Memorial Home with Inspector Saunders' (facing page 106) is a portrait of at least fifteen babies and three nurses in a large drawing room; and 'How Women Police deal with a Lost Child' (facing page 240) is a clumsily posed publicity photograph, where a well-wrapped child is sitting at the side of the road, with Mary seated on a large and shiny motorbike and Margaret Damer Dawson about to climb out of its sidecar.

The Pioneer Policewoman is in effect a sales pitch for women police: this is who we are, forceful authoritative women; this is what we do, cleanse the country of vice and crime; and this is how the public see us, with extraordinary gratitude. Mary refers repeatedly to the way in which a woman in uniform can turn an aggressor into a compliant person through her presence alone. It would appear that the whole country, from guttersnipe to monarch, including pimps and drunkards, is overwhelmed with joy at the arrival of women in policing.

There is a list of the original members of the WPS at the end of the book which interestingly doesn't include Miss Tagart. Despite her loyal attachment to Mary, she only gets a single entry in the index.

Mary's next project was the *Policewoman's Review*, which she founded and edited from 1927 to 1937, inspired by meetings she attended in Europe concerned with the formation of an international body for women police. The remit of the *Policewoman's Review* was to report on the development of women's policing throughout the world, as well as events and progress at home. Much of the content seems to have been written in Mary's own recognisable style, and photographs appear in every issue, often featuring Mary on one of her many foreign trips, in which she is usually accompanied by the retiring figure of Miss Tagart. Her twin concerns – uniforms and morality – are very much to the fore.

The early issues of the *Policewoman's Review* take criticism in good part. The remarks of Ellen Wilkinson MP a vociferous opponent of women police are reported without comment: 'I cannot help wondering sometimes, when one sees those unfortunate policewomen, in their unfortunate uniform, made to look almost like caricatures of male members of the force, whether we shall ever get a really sensible woman brought in to tackle this question.'[1] Although a riposte is expressed in a letter from 'A Ratepayer':

> Why is it only when we come to the Metropolitan women police that we find them turned out as though to make a turn on the stage as the parody of a police-man? The hat is absurd, the boots heavy and ridiculous … May I suggest that a small committee of women, with, say, Commandant Allen in the chair, might evolve a smarter and more suitable uniform, and so be a help to the Commissioner.[2]

Later, an article in the *Evening News* is quoted with great gusto:

> concerning the skirted cop, or policewoman, I do not feel qualified to
> speak: but as a keen lover of beauty I rejoice to learn that their numbers are
> to be substantially increased. A few of these daringly clad sylphs at every
> corner would lend a welcome touch of gaiety to our streets and encourage
> susceptible law-breakers to give themselves up without an invitation.[3]

Here we have one of the many examples of Mary's blindness to mockery.
All publicity is good publicity.

The *Policewoman's Review* is well produced, and includes fiction, poems,
and articles about all sorts of subjects, ranging from animal protection to the
use of clairvoyants by police investigating unsolved crimes. (This is not as
surprising as it may seem; Mary's sister Christine was widely believed to be
a clairvoyant.) Most of the material in the magazine, however, pertains to
policing. In the early days, plenty of advertisers were willing to pay for space
in this widely distributed publication.

In the 1930s Mary's growing concern for the morality of our young
people takes on a sinister turn, when she praises Nazi Germany for taking
action against nudism, which she describes as 'a new form of slavery …
a deeply laid scheme to undermine the natural cleanly [*sic*] and normal
outlook of our youth'.[4] Towards the end of its ten-year life, the tone of the
Policewoman's Review becomes distinctly fascist.

Mary Allen uses the *Policewoman's Review* to praise her own initiative in
founding the Women Police Service (although to be fair, she often refers to
the role of Margaret Damer Dawson). On one occasion she goes so far as to
claim that God has guided her:

> When I look back on the history of our movement since its inauguration
> in 1914 I feel I can say in spite of obstacles and almost insurmountable
> difficulties 'The Lord hath done great things.' I say this in the spirit of
> deepest reverence, for I believe that unless the real guidance of God had
> been acknowledged at the commencement of our work nothing would
> have been accomplished for the good of the race as a whole.[5]

A typical issue (December 1933) contains news from Parliament and the
Magistrates' Association; foreign news (including the closure of disorderly
houses in Hong Kong and Bombay); an article on fingerprints; a short story
called 'Getting a Move On' by Erroll Shaun; an article on the protection of
children in Belgium; a memorial to Margaret Damer Dawson; book reviews;

and an account of a WAS reunion (three pages and four photographs) which includes an encomium from Chief Inspector Campbell, describing Mary Allen in the words of an eighteenth-century song by Henry Carey as:

> *Genteel in personage;*
> *Conduct and equipage;*
> *Noble by heritage,*
> *Generous and free.*

There are several advertisements from, among others, the NSPCC, Maud West: London's Lady Detective, Iona Periford's hair restoration service, and the Au Pair Association. There is also an advertisement for *The Pioneer Policewoman* (5s).

The magazine undoubtedly had an important role in spreading the word about women's policing, at home and abroad, and it was a lifeline for women working in the provinces, giving them news of developments on pay and conditions, and the availability of work. However, it was unable to continue after December 1937. Each issue had become thinner and less lavish, and in the final issue, after a break of some nine months, she expresses her regret for the demise of the paper, saying 'we must have more subscribers'.

A Woman at the Cross Roads, another collaboration with Julie Heyneman, is more about Mary's own philosophy than about policing. It was published in 1934, when Mary's interest in and involvement with fascism was leading her towards membership of Oswald Mosley's British Union of Fascists. Miss Heyneman contributes a chapter on Victorian women, which Mary uses to show how much better standards were in Victorian times than they are in her own. She makes much of the need to combat what she believes to be anti-Christian Communist propaganda, and she makes a statement about the harmful effects of lack of religion:

> Another influence, accountable for the lowering of standards, is the absence of any religious hold on the great majority of modern young women – with no inspiring belief, no stern sense of duty, nor even a consistent theory of life and conduct to take its place … One must have a spiritual history … Prayer is, after all, only formulated aspiration – an expression of inward searching. (p.112)

She draws attention to the problems in society that, in her own opinion, have arisen since the war: 'a fierce desire for new sensations influenced novelists, journalists, dramatists and film producers alike. No immorality was too blatant to be handled in detail, no situation too sordid for exposition.' (p.95) Even 'baby shows' are castigated.

Mary was always a seeker after religious truth, as were her sisters, but for her it is a truth strengthened and guided by strong leadership. She expresses a firm belief in the necessity for a dictatorship:

Dictatorships have, at least, proved that, given some direction they consider really worth while, the youth of each nation is as ready as ever to make sacrifices, and to substitute for all the jargon of 'self-expression', a disciplined control in pursuance of any strong presented national ideal. The very severity of the new regime is found bracing and stimulating, and has brought about the real awakening. (p.143)

Mary deplores so-called 'married women's rights': 'for nine out of ten of the rest of woman-kind, housework is a most wholesome, varied, and diverting occupation, providing them with much-needed physical exercise … Labour-saving devices are excellent in their way, but they free women – to do what?' (p.162) and she concludes that the words 'women's rights' should be replaced with the words 'women's responsibilities'.

Published in the same year as Mary's meeting with Hitler, *A Woman at the Cross Roads* gives a clear indication of the way her philosophy is being shaped by fascism. This encounter is described in some detail in her next and final book, *Lady in Blue*, published in 1936.

Lady in Blue is the most personal of Mary's three volumes of autobiography, describing as it does her own progress from a middle-class home to militant suffragism to police work. It contains accounts of her travels to Germany, Canada, America, Holland, Switzerland, Hungary, Czechoslovakia, Egypt, Greece, Brazil, Uruguay, Finland, Sweden, Denmark, Poland and Palestine: a huge itinerary covered in only about ten years.

The 'Note-Book' which forms the second part of the book is a survey of the causes of crimes, and the solutions she envisages. Among the sources of crime she enumerates are 'foreign undesirables', films, and nudist camps. But she also has something to say about the criminals themselves, and she supports the arguments of the eugenicist, Cesare Lombroso, that criminals are born, not made. She describes the physical characteristics of criminals, and states that 'A great proportion of criminals are left-handed or ambidextrous from childhood,' a conclusion which seems ludicrous today, when children are no longer forbidden to favour their left hand, as they were in Mary's day. She also remarks, without any irony, on the criminal's 'inordinate vanity … a desire to be talked of and noticed.' (p.199)

Parts of *Lady in Blue* were serialised in newspapers, accompanied by lavish illustrations, which did much to boost sales. The book also received a lengthy and effusive review in the *Policewoman's Review* (December 1936). It is unsigned, which casts suspicion on the identity of the reviewer. Could Mary herself have had a hand in its composition? The language is very much like her own: 'On reading the book one has an impression of an indomitable spirit, giving and not counting the cost, fighting and not heeding the wounds, labouring and not asking for reward.' Her restraint and humour are praised: 'We must read between the lines to realise what we are not told in so many words.' The reviewer seems almost to regret that Mary did not take her career even further: 'One cannot refrain from saying "What a diplomatist she would have made!"' This is an extraordinary remark to make about a woman whose lack of tact was notorious, but evidence of the high regard in which she was held by her friends.

Mary was capable of skilful writing which verges on the poetic. She describes a flight over the Midlands during the General Strike:

> in spite of my experience of the English skies, I was extraordinarily impressed, as I passed high over the Black Country, to see a strange and beautiful England spread out below me. For once the great chimneys were idle. Their foul black breath had been blown far and wide by the four winds of Heaven, and below me lay a clean new land that I had never before dreamed of, and that I have never seen since the dark pall of industry has swept down again over it. It was like raising the edge of a curtain that hid a secret country. (p.96)

Mary included writers among her close friends, including the author of *No Surrender* by Jo van Ammers-Küller, who acknowledged Mary's help in supplying 'amusing anecdotes of her work as a "militant"' for her account of a Dutch girl's experiences in London with the WSPU during 1909.[6]

Mary was responsible for the comprehensive WPS Reports of 1919 and 1920, and devised and wrote training programmes for recruits, as well as regulations for their conduct. She wrote prolifically for magazines, about women police, flying[7] and, most of all, the immorality she deplored in the form of nudism and public entertainments. She was an accomplished writer, even if her style was over-ornamented and her subject matter often contentious. Her passion sometimes runs away with her pen, but her handwriting remains as bold and legible as her personality.

WOMEN WILL HAVE TO BE USED

A reunion dinner for members of the Women's Auxiliary Service was held at the Forum Club on 28 October 1933. Most of those present were in uniform, and Mary took the opportunity to announce 'definite plans to form a new Women's Reserve, which, beginning in England and ultimately spreading all over the Empire, would train and drill women for any national emergency (such as the last general strike)'.[1]

The days of the WAS were numbered. Their ranks had been reduced to 150, fifty of whom were in the London area, where the WAS was in conflict with the Metropolitan Police and their now well-established female force. It was a battle Mary knew she had lost. At the same time, the Home Office, who were already showing concern at Mary's self-appointed role as England's leading policewoman, began to take an interest in her political activities.

In December 1933, driven by her belief that war was imminent, as well as by her love of organising women and imposing on them uniforms and military discipline, Mary advertised in the *Policewoman's Review* for recruits to the Women's Reserve, which she had formed in November, convinced that:

> there is not the slightest doubt in the minds of competent military authorities in Europe now, that women will have to be used – and will almost certainly be enlisted for actual work at the Front or with the mechanised columns – in the next great war. Nothing is said about it now, because such statements would serve no useful purpose.[2]

This last sentence is suggestive of the sort of conspiracy theory which undoubtedly pushed Mary towards extreme organisations. She saw the need for 'women pilots to fly the thousands of defensive aeroplanes that will set a ring of guards around our cities. Air and road transport will be vital to this nation.'[3] The paranoia and xenophobia in this statement become even more explicit in the 'call to women' issued in November 1933, in which she speaks of 'subversive teachings,' 'enemies in our midst', and 'poisonous doctrines'. It is an extraordinary statement, passionate to the point of hysteria, comparable in tone and content with the grandiloquent orations of Hitler and Mussolini. Mary claims that, far from being a call to prepare for war, it is asking women to prepare to ensure peace and uphold those ideal of Empire which are threatened by 'the freedom of speech movement … masquerading under the banner of peace'. (*See* Appendix I for full text.)

Mary was so eager to attract large numbers of women to this new organisation that she asked for no subscription fee. How the Women's Reserve was funded remains a mystery, although the wealthy Helen Tagart, who had been Mary's constant companion for many years, was the most likely source. Details of the form and function of the Women's Reserve were outlined in *The Times* of 7 November 1933:

> It is proposed that London shall have 2,000 Women Reservists, trained for duty in the event of any local or national emergency … one of the duties of the Reserves would be a course of instruction in the use of gas masks and in dealing with gas casualties … Although it was not intended to be a military organization, members would wear uniforms consisting of long blue double-breasted coats, with leather belts and berets. Women owning aeroplanes or with cars would be particularly welcomed as members. 'Service for Empire' will be our watchword, and it is hoped that the movement will spread to the Dominions and Colonies.

The Women's Reserve was welcomed by some, including the editor of the *British Journal of Nursing*, Ethel Bedford Fenwick, who is praised to this day for championing the cause of registration for nurses. Mrs Fenwick always supported Mary and her endeavours to keep Britain pure and defend the country from foreign influences. She saw the Women's Reserve as an opportunity for service and training:

> Commandant Mary Allen, head of the Women's Auxiliary Service, is a woman of parts, and over 400 women have joined the new Women's Reserve which she is organising, and which held their first rally recently at the Central Hall, Westminster. The uniform consists of a long double-breasted blue overcoat, a blue beret, and a coloured silk scarf. London detachments will wear buttercup yellow scarves. Green is the colour chosen for Sheffield. Commandant Allen said her ambition was to have

every woman and girl trained along some lines which might be useful to either State departments or municipal authorities in the event of war or civil emergency. They also wished to help to counteract subversive forces. They were not only prepared to serve in the event of war, but prepared to train themselves to be efficient workers in any civil trouble such as the last general strike. They were making training in first aid and training in anti-gas methods and the treatment of gas casualties compulsory.[4]

Mrs Fenwick's admirers might be surprised by the virulence with which she expressed her anti-Semitic views. She writes in the July 1938 issue of the *Journal*:

It seems incredible that our Government is encouraging a flood of German and Austrian Jews into this already congested country, especially as it is well known that a very antagonistic wave of feeling is rising against the swarms of Jews already competing in the labour market in England. Jewish women in England have shown little interest in nursing the sick, as the majority dislike strenuous domestic work of any kind. We hope our sick people will be spared from any such experiment.

This outrageous statement goes beyond anything Mary herself ever committed to print, but its sheer viciousness appears to have done nothing to tarnish Mrs Fenwick's reputation in the history of nursing.

Once again, Mary was putting large numbers of women into uniform, although it is not known who paid for the uniforms. There was no official backing of any sort for the Women's Reserve, nor could there be; for, as R.M. Douglas observes, 'The sole qualification for membership was a disguised racial purity requirement, volunteers being obliged to attest to British nationality and parentage'.[5]

A Home Office Minute, dated 20 November 1933, observes that:

The 'Women's Reserve' would have nothing to do with police, it would apparently function in London and elsewhere as an emergency organisation in times of war or peace, but one of its chief objects appears to be to get ready to combat subversive propaganda. It does not seem that the new baby has got very far yet.[6]

Mary was quick to deny this, sending to the Home Office one of her Women's Reserve leaflets. She states in the accompanying letter, 'I am not considering issuing an appeal for funds as I feel sure these will come privately. I am also not asking for a subscription from members.'[7] The enclosed application form asks for brief particulars of applicants, and does indeed include 'Nationality of Parents'.

On 6 December 1933 we learn from *The Times* that 'Commandant Allen said her ambition was to have every woman and girl trained along some lines which might be useful … in the event of war or civil emergency. They also wished to help to counteract subversive forces.' There would be 'classes for shooting' and 'special classes in preliminary aviation'. This drew a swift and angry response from Lady Londonderry, founder in 1915 of the Women's Legion, a 6,000-strong corps of drivers, cooks and waitresses, who were taken on by the War Department. Lady Londonderry wrote to *The Times* on 7 December, deprecating Mary's plans for a Women's Reserve. She claims that Mary has stated 'that in this new reserve there will be "military rank for officers"' and that it 'would be run, as far as I can see, practically on Fascist lines'. Her object was to 'emphasise in the strongest manner possible that any fresh organization of women, tending towards militarism, is to be deprecated … I do not think it either necessary or desirable at the present moment to start an entirely new organization, which has no recognition from the authorities.'

Lady Londonderry outlined the skills required by the Women's Legion, which were somewhat less dramatic and militaristic than Mary's proposed aviators and shooters. Lady Londonderry suggested that volunteers would be wanted as the more mundane 'cooks, drivers and mechanics, orderlies, clerks, storekeepers, signallers'.[8]

Ramsay Macdonald wrote to the prime minister, complaining that *The Times* letter from Lady Londonderry 'does not in any way purport to represent the views of anyone except herself'.[9] At the same time, Lady Londonderry was making the most of her contacts in government circles. She wrote to Sir John Gilmour suggesting the resuscitation of the Women's Legion. 'It appeared at one time that the Women's Reserve which was being organised by Commandant Allen would be in a position to meet our requirement, but it fails through having no official recognition.'[10] Lady Londonderry's own proposals didn't meet with government approval either. She persisted, writing breathlessly to Sir John Gilmour again on 7 January:

My dear Sir John, Don't consign me to perdition – I have had a brain wave about these – women?? May I bring my plans to you – have nothing in the Press at all to begin with – but may I have a written authorisation from you to quote privately to those individuals from whom I hope to get fat cheques – I feel at the moment rather in a quandary – in view of the letter from the St John's people – turning Allen down – so far have done nothing – if, after I have seen – and you approve the main idea – I would set to work next week and collect some formidable females round me – ready to resist anything.

She ends this letter with an invitation to lunch. It is clear that she hoped that a very personal approach to a friend would win her case. However, Lady Londonderry was discouraged from proceeding with her own scheme, unless she made it clear that it was not approved by the government; but this was quite the opposite of what she wanted, and she put a great deal of pressure on her many personal contacts in the Cabinet. She expresses an intention of discussing the matter with the prime minister, and she writes to Sir John Gilmour on 26 January 1934, questioning what she saw as the secrecy surrounding the question of a women's voluntary force which 'will also militate very much against being able to raise the necessary funds to equip an adequate secretariat, which will be necessary before launching any scheme'. She notes, in some desperation, Mary's success in recruiting large numbers of women; but adds that Mary's scheme has failed through having no official recognition.

Lady Londonderry failed to win her battle for an official launch of her New Women's Legion, which was formed in 1934 and later subsumed into the Women's Auxiliary Defence Service. Her failure to win a government seal of approval left the way open for Mary's Women's Reserve.

Mary was full of optimism, and had ambitious plans. In a pamphlet entitled 'The Women's Reserve: a question and answer' there is the claim that 'members have enrolled in various parts of the Empire. We have started a branch in Montreal, and one will shortly be started in South Africa.'

Mary is persistent. She wrote to Sir John Simon on 15 and 17 June 1935, asking him to see her about the organisation and training of women from 'my Reserve … as ancillaries'; his private secretary wrote to say that he was too busy to see her.

Questions were asked about the legitimacy of the use of firearms. There is clearly some concern about Mary's motives and the people she associates with. On 1 October 1936, it is reported that, 'Miss Allen is said to be a secret adherent of Sir O. Mosley's BUF [British Union of Fascists] and to be in a position to obtain useful information for the Union through her contacts.'[11]

On 13 October 1936, Mary is contacted by letter and advised officially that her organisation would not be of value.

British Pathé has preserved a film clip of Mary launching the first Women's Reserve rally.[12] Mary stands on a platform, in full WAS uniform, with a monocle dangling from a ribbon. She is flanked on her left by gaunt women in Reserve uniform, one of them carrying what looks like a whip. There are about 200 women in the hall, about thirty of them in uniform – greatcoat, beret and scarf, with several apparently well-to-do women in rows behind. Mary speaks from behind a desk:

> If civil emergency arose again, we should have a nucleus of women to whom all the other women who enrolled could be linked up. And instead of wasting time in training we should have women ready, already trained, and we wish to be a body of women ready and able to counteract the subversive forces which without any detail we all of us know are very much alive in our midst today. And our first aim is to show to the world that we have in this country not only women who are prepared to serve in war, but women who are prepared to train themselves to be efficient workers should we again be faced with civil trouble in our midst.

She then comes down to the floor of the hall and inspects the front row, speaking to one of the volunteers in a clipped voice, her posture erect and imposing. The young woman she addresses appears nervous:

Q. Have you enjoyed your drill?
A. Very much, thank you.
Q. And what do you think of the uniform. Do you like it?
A. Yes, very much.
Q. And the scarf. Think it becoming?
A. Very.

Mary travelled the country giving talks and recruiting women. But there was nothing for them to do, and the Women's Reserve ceased to function in December 1939.

When she returned from her 1924 American tour, Mary learned to fly at the Stag Lane aerodrome in Hendon, a popular flying club for would-be pilots. Among her fellow pupils were Lady Bailey and Lady Heath. Amy

Johnson's name is dropped into her account in *Lady in Blue* of her training, as is that of Winifred Spooner, who Mary thought the finest woman pilot, and Sir Alan Cobham. Sir Sefton Brancker, instrumental in organising the Women's Royal Air Force during the war, inspired Mary to form a flying section of the Women's Reserve. 'Obviously, should another war break out, airwomen would be vitally needed, both for communications and for home defence.' Mary claims that the Women's Reserve had access to a number of aircraft: 'In the Women's Reserve we have a number of machines, and some brilliant pilots and potential instructors available in case of any such crisis. Miss Jean Batten is one of our best-known members; and we all belong to the National League of Airmen, and uphold its principles.' (p.38) 'We have members who are Pilots; one has put her aeroplane at Commandant Allen's disposal … A number of our Reservists are qualified air-pilots. Among these are Mrs Battye, Jean Batten and others whose pioneer flights have won the respect of the world. We hope soon to muster several machines of our own. Members of the Aviation Section attend regular lectures and have periodic examinations on the theory of flight. In addition, suitable women are trained as pilots.' (pp.279–80)

Neither Mary Allen nor the Women's Reserve are mentioned in Jean Batten's autobiography, *My Life.*[13]

Mary belonged to the Cinque Ports Flying Club, where her instructor was Captain Sparkes. She made her first solo flight at Stag Lane Aerodrome in 1932. She tells with great relish a story about Lady Heath, who was piloting one day, with Mary as her passenger, and she looped the loop, apparently having forgotten that Mary was not strapped in. Mary is pictured in the 18 January 1934 edition of *Flight* with Mrs E. Battye and two members of the Women's Reserve beside their machine at Reading Aerodrome. (The organisation is wrongly captioned as 'the Women's Auxiliary Service', although the two appear to have shared an address, and perhaps merged into one in Mary's mind, now that the police service was waning.) The only one dressed for flying is Mrs Battye – Mary is in her usual uniform, and the two unnamed women are wearing the uniform overcoats and berets of the Women's Reserve. We are informed that she has appointed Mrs Battye to be her own personal pilot.[14]

Flight Global (1934) reported that:

Some stir was created at the airport on Monday, January 29, when Commandant Mary Allen and Inspector Taggart [*sic*] of the Women's Auxiliary Force, left for Berlin by the D.L.H. 10 am service, in order, it is averred, to interview Herr Hitler on questions relating to the status of women in the world at large and in Germany in particular. The ladies left Croydon in full uniform, including field boots, military-style caps and (one) a monocle. Knowing Herr Hitler's ideas about women, the hearth, home and all that, the interview should be an interesting one.

Stephen Dorril has described 'the airman myth – a key component of Fascist thought – [which] incorporated "idealised visions of war and youth with futurist revolutionary ideas"'.[15] This is undoubtedly part of Mary's inspiration for the airborne component of the Women's Reserve. However, not all pro-Nazi aviators agreed that women should become pilots. C.G. Gray wrote scathingly in *The Aeroplane* in 1941:

We quite agree that there are millions of women in the country who could do useful jobs in war. But the trouble is that so many insist on wanting to do jobs which they are quite incapable of doing. The menace is the woman who thinks she ought to be flying a high speed bomber when she really has not the intelligence to scrub the floor of a hospital properly, or who wants to nose around as an Air Raid Warden and yet can't cook her husband's dinner.

13

A HITLER OF THE SPIRIT

In 1934 Mary Allen wrote in *A Woman at the Cross Roads*: 'There seems no question that a recent speaker was right who proclaimed that the need of the world today is "A Hitler of the Spirit".' (p.159) She does not give us the identity of the speaker she quotes; but it is known that in the same year Mary asked for and was granted an audience with Hitler in Germany.

Mary began her association with a series of charismatic fascist men in 1926, when she met Eion O'Duffy, the leader of the Irish Blueshirts, at the International Police Congress in Berlin:

> One of the most interesting personalities at the Conference was General O'Duffy, representing the Irish Free State Police. It was said to be over a disagreement concerning the powers of the police that General O'Duffy later quarrelled with Mr de Valera, with the result that the Blue Shirt Movement in Ireland, which had been described as a sort of private police system, was broken up.[1]

This is a somewhat disingenuous description of O'Duffy's organisation; Mary is unlikely to have been ignorant of the fact that the Blueshirts were modelled on Germany's Nazis, with marches, flags and a 'Hail O'Duffy' salute.

Mary had visited Germany in an official capacity many times; first in June 1923, when she was requested by the government to report on the potential for women police to cope with problems of 'vice and increasing disease'[2] associated with the British Army on the Rhine (*see* Chapter 8). She returned to Germany in June 1925, having been invited to attend the International Exhibition of Police Institutions and Work in Karlsruhe. She then travelled to Basle and Vienna, where she met Johann Schober, Police President of Austria, who later became Chancellor of Austria ('a most charming and gifted man'³). Schober invited Mary to attend the International Police Congress and Exhibition in Berlin in 1926.

Mary returned to Germany in January 1934 'just after the burning of the Reichstag Building in Berlin and the great Nazi development'. German policewomen had ceased to function when Hitler came to power because it was 'riddled with Communist propaganda' and Mary wanted 'to see whether a new force of Women Police could not be built up in accordance with Nazi principles'.⁴ She is unequivocal in her praise for Hitler: 'For two and a half hours I sat absolutely entranced beside the Chancellor's charming sister, listening to the great Dictator ... this man's hypnotic gestures, his passionate, forceful voice and his visionary eyes held me spellbound.'⁵ She saw in him 'an enduring friend of England, and a blood-brother of the ordinary decent people of Europe'. In a museum of Communist exhibits collected by the German police, she was horrified by 'all sorts of incredibly foul and blasphemous pamphlets scoffing at religion, decency [and] home life ... Hitler and no one else is the barrier holding back the tide of Communism from Western Europe.' An effusive description of her own meeting with Hitler leaves no doubt as to her admiration not just for the man, but also for Nazi ideology. She did not share the sexual attraction described by other English gentlewomen who met him, such as Diana and Unity Mitford. Mary was a confirmed lesbian. Her adulation of Hitler was for 'a man after her own heart' who she believed to be one of the greatest orators who ever lived. She writes vividly of the emotional reception he received from war veterans and youth organisations; of his love of music; and of his ruthless weeding out of the enemies of the Reich. She finds him utterly without fault.

Mary was entirely convinced by Hitler's anti-Communist arguments. 'If we want street fighting and mass murder in England, the surest way to attain it is to continue the hysterical anti-Hitler propaganda in which certain of our newspapers have recently been indulging.'⁶

Mary also visited Germany to attend the notorious Nazi Olympic Games in Berlin in 1936, but she left no record of her impressions of this extraordinary event. She was to claim later that she had hardly any first-hand knowledge of Germany, but it is clear that she visited several times and spoke German well enough not to need the assistance of an interpreter in her interview with Hitler.

Mary was connected to fascist organisations at home by friends and acquaintances. A number of WAS members joined the British Union of

Fascists, including Inspector More Nisbett, a WAS officer described by Mary Allen as 'one of its ablest speakers',[7] who claimed that her experience as a WAS officer showed her the need for a fascist 'holy war': 'one had only to walk the streets or go into the public-houses … or to mix with the people who frequented the courts, to realise how very real the Red peril was.'[8]

It is perhaps necessary to remind ourselves that many establishment figures were intimately associated with the radical right, including the Home Secretary from November 1924 to June 1929, Sir William Joynson-Hicks. In the Home Office dossier on Mary Allen, Joynson-Hicks repeatedly rejects requests from the commissioner of the Metropolitan Police to investigate or prosecute her. In a letter dated 16 August 1927, he writes:

> With regard to Miss Allen's activities generally, the Secretary of State is not at present aware of anything which appears to give ground for serious concern, but if you find evidence of conduct which is an infringement of the law or otherwise contrary to the public interest, he will at any time be prepared to consider any steps you may think it necessary to recommend.[9]

The correspondence in question related to the Freemantle affair (*see* Chapter 9), in which Mary was alleged to have impersonated a Metropolitan Police officer and compiled a dossier on a woman she suspected of procuring abortions. There can be no doubt that Joynson-Hicks was in a position to protect Mary, and that he chose to do so.

Although it is possible to detect loose associations between fascist organisations and the Women's Auxiliary Service, in that many women were members of both, links between the suffragette movement and fascism are also discernible. Mary's own *documented* involvement with British fascism begins in 1939; but she was undoubtedly mingling with women who went on to become British Union of Fascists (BUF) stalwarts in the thirty years since she left home to join the women's suffrage movement.

Two of the few ex-suffragettes who became active members of the BUF have interesting histories. Like Mary, Norah Elam and Mary Richardson both endured repeated force-feeding in prison; and each stood unsuccessfully for Parliament.

Norah Elam was arrested three times in 1914, and jailed in Holloway. At this time, she was known by her first husband's name, Dacre-Fox. Her most dramatic arrest was made outside Westminster Abbey, where she had interrupted a sermon by the Bishop of London, calling for him to stop the force-feeding of suffragettes. An Anglican nun covered Mrs Dacre-Fox's mouth with a handkerchief, and led her outside the Abbey, where she was arrested. In the same year, she stood unsuccessfully for Parliament as an Independent candidate in Richmond, Surrey.

As early as 1918, Mrs Dacre-Fox's activities were being reported in the malignant Mrs Fenwick's *British Journal of Nursing*:

> Mrs Dacre-Fox, the organiser of the enthusiastic mass meeting held in Trafalgar Square last Saturday in support of a 'clean sweep' of Germans at large and in office, had reason to be well satisfied with the spirited determination it evinced. The speakers used good old Saxon English, and the following resolution was passed with loud and prolonged acclamations: 'That this mass meeting regards the proposals made by the Home Secretary on Thursday in the House of Commons as futile and useless to deal with the alien enemy, and refuses to accept any such compromise on the part of the authorities.' It demands the immediate internment of all aliens of enemy blood, whether naturalised or unnaturalised, the removal of all such aliens from every Government and public office, and calls upon the Government to take whatever steps are necessary to put this resolution into effect.
>
> When the resolution was carried, Mrs. Dacre-Fox said she would ask the Prime Minister to receive a deputation in order to convey to him the determination of the meeting to see that no half-measures were adopted by the Government in the treatment of the enemy alien peril.[10]

Dacre-Fox later joined the Conservative Party, defecting to the BUF in 1934 with her second husband, Dudley Elam. Nora Elam took a prominent role in the BUF, and she enjoyed the dubious distinction of being the only ex-suffragette interned by the British Government under Defence Regulation 18B, in May 1940.

Mary Richardson, famous for slashing a painting in the National Gallery, the Rokeby Venus, with a hatchet, also stood for Parliament, but as a Labour Party candidate. She lost to three Conservative candidates (in Acton in 1922 and 1924, and in Aldershot in 1931). Her career is more complex than Nora Elam's. Her prison experience made her into a socialist; yet she joined Mosley's BUF and became organising secretary of the Women's Section in April 1934, writing in the fascist weekly, *The Blackshirt*:

> I was first attracted to the Blackshirts because I saw in them the courage, the action, the loyalty, the gift of service, the ability to serve which I had known in the suffragette movement. When later I discovered that the

Blackshirts were attacked for no visible cause or reason, I admired them the more when they hit back, and hit hard.[11]

It would be a mistake to see Nora Elam, Mary Richardson and Mary Allen as following typical post-suffrage careers in becoming fascists. They were in fact unusual for doing so, and their actions are perhaps indicative more of their own personality types than of a natural progression from one cause to the other.

❧❧

The Home Office, which was already showing concern at Mary's self-appointed role as England's leading policewoman, began to take an interest in her political activities after the departure of the protective Joynson-Hicks. The new Home Secretary, John Robert Clynes, notes that 'some of her activities have been rather on the questionable side';[12] but it is not until the end of 1933 that her political motives are questioned.

The Home Office dossier on Mary Allen first mentions her name in connection with fascism on 5 January 1934,[13] when reference is made to a report of a visit by Miss Allen to the headquarters of the British Fascists to obtain particulars of the people in key positions in the electrical and gas undertakings in London.

By 1936, Mary's association with fascism became a subject for real concern at the Home Office: 'Miss Allen is said ... to be a secret adherent of Sir O. Mosley's BUF and to be in a position to obtain useful information for the Union through her contacts.'[14]

There were also concerns about Mary's activities in Franco's Spain. The *Sydney Morning Herald* of 18 January 1937 reported:

A message from Salamanca reports that Commandant Mary Allen formerly of the London women police, visited the insurgent headquarters after a week's tour. Commandant Allen, who was wearing riding breeches and boots, and a peaked cap, said she had been invited to visit Spain to see if there was scope for women police. She expressed the opinion that Spanish women politically were better informed than the women of other countries, and should, therefore, make fine policewomen.

And in the *Policewoman's Review* of 6 March 1937, it is reported that, 'Commandant Allen has just returned from Spain, where she was invited by General Franco a month or two ago to see if it were politic to form a force of women police in that country'.

Mary did indeed write about conditions for women in Spain. The *Catholic Herald* praised her efforts: 'After visiting Spain in 1937 at the invitation of General Franco, Commandant Allen addressed many meetings to give first-hand information on conditions after the Civil War. At one of these meetings the late Archbishop Amigo, Bishop of Southwark, paid her a warm tribute for her courage in raising her voice on behalf of a suffering Church which at that time she had no thought of joining.'[15] Mary was also a speaker at a pro-Franco meeting organised by the Friends of National Spain in the Usher Hall, Edinburgh on 18 June 1938. A resolution congratulating General Franco and the Spanish people on their heroic and successful fight to maintain Christian civilisation, freedom, and religion in Spain, was carried on the motion of Commandant Mary Allen. 'Franco has won,' she declared.[16]

In a note to the Home Office (date-stamped June 1940), Mr G.B. Hamilton, a journalist with a special interest in fascism, reported that he had seen a dossier on Mary compiled by del Vayo, a Spanish Republican politician and journalist. 'He drew my attention to the fact that, in his estimation, this lady was Franco's most dangerous agent in Great Britain … Miss Allen is unquestionably a political character and would I imagine provide the most classical example possible of a "Fifth Columnist".' According to del Vayo's dossier, Mary visited Spain on numerous occasions when she was:

> always promptly received by the Caudillo himself … Miss Allen had made complete arrangements with the British Fascist Party and its sympathisers to stage meetings of protest, if and when the British Government showed any symptoms of sympathy for the Republicans … On one occasion Miss Allen went from Burgos to Lisbon … on a mission which Franco himself entrusted to her.[17]

Mary denied having met Franco at all when interviewed by the Home Office Advisory Committee:

Q. You went to Spain, I see?
A. Yes.
Q. Was that during the Civil War?
A. Yes; in 1937.
Q. You went several times, did you?
A. Only once. We were only invited once.
Q. You met General Franco?
A. No, I did not meet General Franco. We were his guests. He knew we were there.

Q.   You did not visit him on numerous occasions?

A.   No. Good gracious, no. He was at the front. He was at Madrid.[18]

She persists in her denial of ever having met Franco, and claims that the visit was 'in order to enquire into the activities of the women and whether they were going to have women police'.

But it was not until 1940 that these privately held suspicions receive public confirmation, and internment is being considered a real possibility. In an undated Home Office memo it is stated that:

> Little information seems to be available on her activities from 1936 until April 1940 … During and immediately after the war of 1914–1918 she did good and valuable work in the national interest: but after she ceased to hold any official appointment she somehow contrived by her demeanour, by her dress, and by her behaviour, to make it appear to the public of this and other countries that she was still acting in some official capacity … It was and is considered that Miss Allen was sufficiently active in the furtherance of the objects of the BUF to justify her detention. It is most improbable, in the case of a person of her character, that her activities were limited to those which were discovered by the vigilance of the police … it is the view of the HO that it would be contrary to the national interest to permit Miss Allen, in view of her past conduct and her expressed views, to be at liberty under any less stringent conditions.[19]

Mary was ready to speak openly about her political persuasion. On 26 April 1940 it was reported in the *Daily Mirror* that an MP was asking questions in the House about Mary: 'Whether he is aware that Commandant Mary Allen is a member of the British Union of Fascists, spoke on Sir Oswald Mosley's platform at Friends House on April 13, and is contributing a series of articles to *Action*.'

> When the *Daily Mirror* spoke to Miss Allen at her West Country home last night she said: 'How can the Secretary for War discharge me when I am not working for him? The Women's Voluntary Service is not active at the moment. I do not belong to any Government body. In the years I have been running my auxiliary service I have trained thousands of women to do patriotic work for their country. Since the war I have done nothing. Why should I? I have not been asked to train any women although I feel I should have been. As regards the question of my political views, I say quite openly that I am a member of the Fascist Party. I joined the

party just over a month ago, but that does not make me any the less patriotic. I would work for my country tomorrow – training women for the Services – if I was asked. I did speak at a meeting at which Sir Oswald Mosley was present, but it was a women's peace meeting. I certainly said nothing unpatriotic.'[20]

In a *News Chronicle* interview on 27 April she goes further: 'It is true that I am a member of the British Union. I joined the Union a month or so ago because I believe that we should have a negotiated peace now. That does not mean to say that I am a pacifist or a pro-Nazi.' And she tells the *Daily Telegraph* on 26 April 1940:

> It was at a women's peace meeting at the Friends' House that I spoke on April 13. Neither Germany nor politics was mentioned. The articles [in *Action*] referred to are the result of a letter I wrote to the *Daily Telegraph* on stage nudity. There is no suggestion of politics in the series.

She told the *Daily Herald*, also on 26 April, 'Any political views I have expressed since the outbreak of war have been as a private citizen. I have closed my office in Victoria street, made no further attempt to collect voluntary funds to finance my organization [the Women's Reserve] – in fact it is suspended for the duration.'

Mary did indeed write a series of articles on vice for the BUF newspaper, *Action*. She had long been obsessed with what she called 'sex crime', to which she devotes a whole chapter in *Lady in Blue*. Gottlieb notes that 'The BUF's women's policy did highlight certain areas of anti-Semitic discourse, and particularly rampant were stereotypes of the predatory Jew exploiting women workers in the sweatshops, perpetrating sex crimes, and disseminating indecent literature.'[21] There was also a movement within the BUF to condemn Jews because of their methods of killing animals. Meetings of prominent fascists were held at the home of Mrs Dacre-Fox, who ran the London and Provincial Anti-Vivisection Society, which Thurlow describes as 'a known fascist front organization'.[22] (Margaret Damer Dawson, Mary's lover and co-founder of the Women Police Service was a noted worker for animal protection, Secretary of the International Congress of Animal Protection Societies, and recipient of numerous awards in this field. There were a number of anti-vivisection societies in London and elsewhere, most of which were genuinely dedicated to the protection of animals.)

In her *Action* articles, Mary blamed what she called 'the vice racket' on 'the influence of refugees from the Continent' (she seems to forget that in 1925 she described Belgian refugees sympathetically in *The Pioneer Policewoman* as 'that piteous invasion' (p.9) and recommended 'the total elimination of all foreigners engaged in the abominable trade'. These remarks sit uneasily with her declarations that her contributions to *Action* were *only* about vice and not political at all.

Evidence that Mary associated with prominent BUF members comes from a letter she wrote on 30 April 1940 to Captain Ramsay, which was found when he was arrested in May 1940:

> Dear Captain Ramsay, I feel I must write to you at once and thank you for your most remarkable and immediate help to me today. I cannot tell you how deeply grateful I am, for I did not even dare to hope you would be able to get the question withdrawn. My joy was, and is, very real! One more victory over the enemy which makes one more hopeful of ultimate success. I thank you again – Yours sincerely, Mary Allen

The identity of 'the enemy' is not specified. In fact, Mary's enemies were many. Members of the public were eagerly coming forward to label her a Nazi, including a Miss Cecily Fraser, a journalist who had seen Mary with a view to getting a story from her. She was 'terribly struck by Commandant Allen's Fascist sympathies. She said that Miss Allen had expressed her admiration for the Gestapo and Himmler and had more or less said that she would help the Germans if they came here.'[23] Another witness wrote to the Home Secretary on 14 June 1940:

> In January 1938 I was staying at the Schweizerhof Hotel, Kandersteg, Switzerland, and Miss Mary Allen and her sister were staying in the same hotel. I consider it my duty to inform you that she stated on many occasions that she was a personal friend of Hitler's and expressed the greatest admiration for him. PS. At the same time a young man whose name I do not remember, held exactly the same views and discussed Hitler at dinner time every evening with Miss Allen. Both he and Miss Allen spoke fluent German. I do remember that he was the son of a Chief Constable in the Birmingham district and feel that you should know this.[24]

Perhaps most damning was the information provided by a member of the Kent County Constabulary:

> I interviewed Major J. Dupe, Head of Staff at Lympne Airport, he said 'I know both Miss Allen and Miss Tagart. With ref to Miss Allen, she has

travelled to Germany frequently and always returned by a German air-craft. She always gave the Nazi salute to the pilot on alighting. During the last war she served in occupied territory and made German friends. She is a great believer in Spiritualism and is involved in Freemasonry … Miss Tagart always accompanied her on her various trips.' I [also] interviewed Mrs Bradley [and] she said 'I was cook at Danehill with Miss Allen and Miss Tagart for eighteen years … I cannot definitely say if she is a friend of Field-Marshal Goering. She used to run a Nursing Home on Hythe sea front but gave that up … Mrs Bradley admitted to me that she thought a lot of Miss Allen, also that she was being careful of what she said to me, for fear of any consequences as regards getting into any trouble.'[25]

There is no concrete evidence that Mary actually made her rumoured secret visits to Germany at the invitation of SS Chief Heinrich Himmler, and she always denied such allegations; which of course she would have done, had they been true. Such rumours are as hard to disprove as they are to prove. As for Nazi salutes to German pilots, when questioned about this she replied: 'I may go like that, and raise my hand when I say goodbye, but I really doubt that I would do it to the pilot unless I happened to know him.' And in answer to the remark 'the Nazi salute is not like our salute; it is done much more with the outstretched arm,' she says, 'I have never dreamt of such a thing'.[26]

A number of MPs were agitating for internment, and Special Branch submitted a report on 25 June 1940, claiming that Mary had been:

an active adherent of the British Union of Fascists for some years, although she did not take any open part until about the end of 1939. Prior to that time, her connection with the movement was kept a closely guarded secret, because it was considered that she was in a position to gain valuable information for the BUF.[27]

The same report listed her fascist contacts, including Margaret Bothamley, believed to be living in Germany and working with the German Government on broadcasts in English, Lady Domvile, Aubrey Lees, Captain Ramsay, Nora Elam, and Muriel Whinfield (the last two had been interned).

At this time, Mary was living in a house near St Just in Cornwall, where the police were keeping a close watch on her, and reported that she was 'lying very low'.[28]

A question about Mary was asked in the House of Commons on 27 June 1940:

> *Mr Glenvil Hall* asked the Home Secretary whether Miss Mary Allen still represents the Women's Auxiliary Service on the Advisory Council of Women's Voluntary Services for Civil Defence, set up under the auspices of his Department?
>
> *Sir J. Anderson* I am informed that, when the Women's Voluntary Services for Civil Defence came into being two years ago at the request of my predecessor in office, the Women's Auxiliary Service was one of a large number of voluntary organisations invited to be represented on the Advisory Council. I understand that this organisation has, in fact, been represented on a number of occasions in the past by Miss Mary Allen, but that neither she nor any other representative of the Women's Auxiliary Service has attended a meeting of the Council since January last.
>
> *Mr Hall* May I take it from that answer that this lady will not be asked to further meetings and that she is to be interned, in view of the facts that she has boasted openly that she is a Fascist and proud of it, and that she is now living on the coast?[29]

No satisfactory answer was forthcoming, and a further question was asked in the House of Commons on 4 July 1940: 'To ask the Secretary of State for the Home Department if he will give an assurance that neither Miss Mary Allen nor any other representative of the WAS will be permitted to attend future meetings of the Women's Voluntary Services for Civil Defence', which seemed to provoke the Home Office into serious consideration of detention under Defence Regulation 18B(1A). After some interdepartmental argument, it was concluded that Mary was not sufficiently dangerous to warrant internment, and that imposing restrictions on her movements would be more appropriate, and an order was made on 11 July 1940, and suspended under 18B(2) on the same date.

The reasons given for the order were as follows:

1. The Secretary of State had reasonable cause to believe that you have been a member of the organisation known as British Union, or have been active in the furtherance of its objects and that it is necessary to exercise control over you
2. At the time of the Order made against you the Secretary of State had reasonable cause to believe that you had been or were a member of

the British Union which was an organisation of the kind referred to in Regulation 18B(1A) …

Particulars. You, the said Mary Allen:-
1. were an active member of the British Union
2. were an associate of active members and of leaders of the British Union
3. have attended and addressed meetings held in support of the British Union
4. have expressed pro-German views
5. are of doubtful loyalty to this country.

The conditions of the order imposed on Mary were: to continue to reside at St Just in Cornwall; not to travel more than 5 miles therefrom without the Chief Constable of Cornwall's permission; to notify her movements to the police weekly; not to have or use any private motor vehicle, bicycle, telephone or wireless transmitting or receiving set; to observe a curfew.

Mary objected to these conditions, and 6 November was set as the date for her appeal against them to be heard at the Berysted Hotel in Ascot.

14

YELLOW AND WHITE FLOWERS

When the Detention Order was served, Mary's home in Nanquidno Valley in Cornwall was searched. (For a transcript of the Police Officers' account of the search and service, see Appendix II.) She had had the house built for her in a remote area about seven years previously, and lived there with Helen Tagart and various dogs.

The police officers who attended were Acting Detective Sergeant Martin (the author of the report), Sergeant Penhaligon and Detective Constable Roberts. When Mary had been formally served, she remarked to DS Martin that she had an injured knee, and would therefore be unable to walk to the police station at St Just to notify her movements. Martin replied with breathtaking sarcasm that 'if she could not walk she would have no movements to report'.

Among the items found in the house were membership cards of the British Union of Fascists, in the names of Mary S. Allen and Helen Bourn Tagart; copies of *Action*; and three anti-Semitic pamphlets. These constitute damning evidence that refutes Mary's claims that her membership of the BUF was neither political nor motivated by anti-Semitism.

Mary is bad-tempered and devious throughout the interview with the Advisory Committee at Ascot on 6 November 1940, refusing to answer some questions, saying that she cannot remember the correct answers to others, answering with questions of her own, changing her story from one minute to the next, and juggling with dates. Sometimes her language is so convoluted that it is hard to make sense of what she is saying. Whether or not this is deliberate, it is certainly effective in tying her interrogators in knots. But she is very firm in her denial of unpatriotic behaviour.

She begins by questioning the restrictions imposed on her:

> I am not objecting to restrictions as such, if they have to be put on, but
> I am objecting to any restrictions at all, because I do not consider I deserve
> them. I would not dream of objecting to restrictions as laid down for a
> certain office, but when you have not committed the offence you are in
> rather a different position.[1]

The chairman tries to mollify Mary by asking her to tell him something
about herself, questions she brushes aside with her customary acerbity. She
denies being an active member of the British Union, saying that she joined
in December 1939, and spoke at one meeting. She claims that, as far as she is
concerned, 'the British Union was and is for the British Empire' and aimed
to keep the Empire out of the war; and that she and the union were in favour
of a negotiated peace. She no longer favours a negotiated peace so, according
to her own logic, the restrictions placed on her should not now apply.

Asked about the Women's Reserve, Mary says they were 'working full
blast' for the government up to November 1939. 'No one knew I had any
Fascist sympathies – or British Union sympathies, I prefer to call them
– because we did not speak about politics.'[2] This admission of fascist sympathies seems to be a slip of the tongue. She denies such sympathies elsewhere;
but it is not taken up by the interviewer.

Asked about visits to Germany, Mary describes her work with policewomen in Cologne, and then answers questions about her meeting with
Hitler. 'I found Hitler's speech remarkable. I do not understand very much
German, but I heard his first speech in the Reichstag … As an orator,
I thought he was extraordinary.'[3] The interviewer questions her about her
impressions of Hitler as described in *Lady in Blue*, but Mary brushes this
aside, and claims not to have seen him since, and to have no opinion about
him now. She is not picked up on the blatant lie about her understanding of
the German language.

It is explained to Mary that the BUF is a banned organisation by order of
the Home Secretary, and that a member of it can be detained if it is necessary to exercise control. She insists that she was an inactive member, and
that therefore detention should not apply to her. 'I have been a member of
social clubs, but not political ones.'[4]

On the restrictions to her movements, Mary describes herself as 'a
prisoner in my own house' and complains of the indignity of being seen
reporting to the police when she had been a policewoman herself for so
many years.

She insists that she has not met General Franco ('I wish I had') and that she only met Hitler on one occasion, and that she has not visited Germany since. She is anxious to have the endorsement removed from her identity card, and the chairman goes so far as to suggest that she might lose it, and apply for a replacement.

Predictably, Mary comes alive when she is questioned about her uniform, which seems to be as much of an obsession with the committee as it once was with the Metropolitan Police. Towards the end, the chairman of the interview committee says:

Q.   You know, that uniform that you wear worries me.

A.   Does it? I have worn it so many years.

Q.   I cannot help thinking that it is at the bottom of a lot of this trouble. You do not mind my saying that?

A.   Not a bit. But I cannot take it in. If you have earned a thing, and worn it for so many years, 25 years, you do not consider yourself in that way – whether you have it on or not.

Q.   I see that it has become part of you?

A.   It is part of me. Everybody knows it. I am not afraid of wearing it, even though everyone might say: 'There goes a Fascist.' That does not affect me.

Q.   I do not think it is that. I should say, when I saw the uniform: 'There is a high official in the Women's Police Force.' That is the impression I should have.

A.   I consider that that is what I ought to have had.

Q.   But you must not dress according to what you consider. Many of us think we ought to have wings on our backs.

A.   Yes; but I did begin the Women's Police and I did train them and have been training them ever since.

Q.   We are talking very frankly. Are you quite sure it is not a mistake?

A.   That, of course, I cannot agree. At the moment, as I am not doing anything, I do not wear it in Cornwall.

Q.   You do not wear it in Cornwall?

A.   There is nothing to wear it for, in the country.

Q.   You do not necessarily put it on every day?

A.   Good heavens, no. But I had to come to London to see you, and I must dress like I always do when I come to London.

Q.   I think we should have infinitely preferred to see you dressed as you generally are, and not as you are today. It is another matter if you were doing work as an ambulance driver.

A.   But I hope to be doing some more work.

Q.   Do you think you are walking about dressed up like a kind of women's field marshal?

A.   That is all right. I consider I have worked for it and I have created it.

Q.   I think there is a lot to be said for it, but you have to remember the sort of world that you and I live in, and the sort of thing people say and think. In time of war, I suppose people may not like anybody who is not in an official position going about looking as if they were a sort of female field marshal.

A.   As soon as I am free I shall be doing some work, whether it is as a field marshal or whatever it may be. There is nothing to make me remain where I am except these restrictions. There is plenty of work that I can do and plenty of work where my uniform will be absolutely useful to me.

…

Q.   Do they [the members of the Women's Auxiliary Service] all have that bright red lining?

A.   No; they have not all got that; not the red silk.[5]

A copy of a Variation Order suspending the operation of the Detention Order was served on Mary by the Cornwall Constabulary on 13 January 1941. Three wireless receiving sets were returned to her. Under this new order, the conditions of weekly reporting to the police, curfew and some of the restrictions on equipment were lifted so that she would be allowed to use a bicycle. Mary was not satisfied with this, and promptly demanded that all restrictions be lifted, but she was informed that the Secretary of State was not prepared to make any further variation of the order. She applied again a year later, and the chief constable did allow her to visit Penzance to go shopping. She was, however, still of interest to the Home Office and MI5.

The Home Office examined letters which were exchanged in September and October 1942 between Miss Tagart, Miss Abbott (an old friend of Mary's from her suffragette days) and Lilian Barker, who also knew Mary as a suffragette ('Allen always loved the limelight').[6] Helen Tagart was hoping that something could be done for Mary, and she deplored the accusations made by 'enemies and fanatics'. We learn that Helen was present at Mary's interview with Hitler, and she also alleges that a camera and revolver were confiscated when Mary's house was searched, although these items are not mentioned in the report of the police search of 10 July 1940.

Helen writes with passion and loyalty. 'They can find no better use for such outstanding capabilities and experience as the Commandant possesses than to stamp on them as hard as possible.'[7] The report on these letters concedes that, 'The conditions to which she is subject are more severe than those commonly applied to persons who have actually been detained under 18B and since released under a suspending direction'.[8]

However, there was still considerable suspicion about Mary's activities, and in a letter to the Chief Constable of Cornwall dated 12 May 1943, marked Secret, E.A. Airy (unidentified) wrote:

Miss Allen's companion Helen Taggart [*sic*] wrote to Mrs Dudley Elam on the 30th April last. Mrs Elam was a very prominent member of the BUF, who was detained for some time but was eventually released on compassionate grounds to look after her sick husband. Miss Taggart wrote to her 'we should be so glad (the C especially) to hear a report of that meeting if you have got it yet. We have thought so much about it and were with you in spirit all that day. [I] am sure you will sympathise with our longing to hear ... I wish we had some of those yellow and white flowers to send you that the C. used to send but we cannot get them now.' The 'C' stands, I presume, for Commandant. The meeting to which Miss Taggart refers is probably one of those held under the auspices of the 18B Publicity Council. The underlining is written by Miss Taggart. I should be interested if you are able to throw any light on the strange sentence about the yellow and white flowers.[9]

If the mystery about the yellow and white flowers was ever solved, the answer remains a secret. It is easy to be misled, when reading someone else's letters, and to find something that isn't there; but in view of the fact that the recipient was the previously interned Nora Elam, the writer's suspicions are understandable.

Throughout July and August 1943, Mary is still applying for removal of all restrictions, and there is general agreement that 'in spite of her ability [she] is a spent force'.[10] But she is still on the suspect list, and kept under observation. She is now living in London, and MI5 are informed of her presence there.

By November 1944 the patience of the authorities has reached its limit. 'It seems incredible that this woman still does not understand the condition to which she is subject'; she is 'being as awkward as possible' to the police; and 'it would save a great deal of trouble to everybody to cancel the order' and monitor her movements through the National Registration authorities.[11]

Mary's persistence in making a thorough nuisance of herself finally paid off. A Revocation Order was signed by the Secretary of State on 28 November 1944. She was free at last.

❧ ☙

Mary continued her association with Mosley, and was photographed with him in 1948, when she was 70 years old. Her cropped hair has grown a couple of centimetres, but underneath her overcoat, she is still wearing masculine clothes with a necktie and a hint of uniform about them. This is the last known documentation of Mary until notices of her death appear in the newspapers in 1964.

Lady in Blue ends with a call to arms as passionate as any made by the male fascists Mary had come to love and admire:

> From the Orkneys to Land's End our members come, representing every rank and profession, a mighty and increasing sisterhood standing patiently and steadfastly together, seeking no gain, asking no recognition, content to wait for that time in the dim future when the safety of nations and the sanity of the world may depend on those of its women who have waited with lamps trimmed and clearly burning in the gathering darkness of the war-clouds. (p.282)

15

HELEN'S LOSS HAS TAKEN
AWAY ALL JOY IN LIFE

Mary Allen had left the public stage by the end of the Second World War. Always a private person, her home life is less easy to piece together than her well-documented activities as a suffragette, policewoman, world traveller and fascist sympathiser.

In 1945, she was 67 years old, and apparently in poor health, although she lived for another nineteen years. She was well enough to continue to act as a judge at Crufts Dog Show until 1952. Mary had always been a dog-lover, and shared her home with a variety of breeds, as well as breeding Pekingese and St Bernards. She was most famous for her prize-winning 'Sherhill' Pekingese dogs, exhibited at Crufts throughout the 1930s and 1940s, one of which, Champion Chu-Fuan of Sherhill, was much photographed. Posters of him are still on sale all over the world today.

Mary made a number of firm and enduring friendships in the early days. Many of her suffragette colleagues followed her into policing, including Isobel (Toto) Goldingham, who became one of the WPS's Council of Three with Mary and Margaret Damer Dawson.

When Miss Goldingham asked the government to give a further honour to Mary in recognition of her first-war work, particularly that in connection with the army on the Rhine, it was noted in the Home Office file that:

> Miss Allen has the OBE already – it was given to her in 1918 for war work – so Miss Goldingham no doubt has a CBE in mind. So far as HO is concerned there is, I take it, nothing doing. Miss Allen's enthusiasm is constantly outrunning her discretion … and only quite recently the

National Council of Women have been moved to resent her habit of passing herself off as a sort of Chief Policewoman.[1]

It was Toto Goldingham, who died in 1957 in Tonbridge, who introduced Mary to Radclyffe Hall, the novelist famous for her openly lesbian life and novels:

> One of their close friends was a Miss Goldingham, whom they called Toto. Through the latter they were introduced to another curious pair, Commandant Mary Allen (known as Robert) and her companion Miss Taggart [*sic*], who lived at a house in Lympne called 'Danehill' with two St Bernards. Robert Allen had been a militant suffragette ... and helped found the Women's Volunteer Police Force during the war, subsequently becoming its Commandant. After the war, however, despite her protestations, the Home Office disbanded the organization and it had since existed in an unofficial capacity only, kept alive largely by the efforts of Miss Allen who was never happier than when wearing her uniform and highly polished boots. It seemed unlikely that the force would ever be resurrected and the dejected Commandant was reduced to hoping that coal or transport strikes might lead to a call upon her services. John and Una [Radclyffe Hall and her companion, Una Troubridge] sympathised, agreeing that the authorities were against her because she was an invert (all they wanted, Una declared contemptuously, were 'fluffy policewomen'). The two couples were heartened to find that they shared common beliefs on the subject of homosexuality.[2] ... Robert Allen and Miss Taggart came for lunch of December 23, the Commandant appearing in 'mufti' – pale fawn breeches, a scarlet golf coat and patent leather pumps.[3]

Mufti is clearly unusual dress for Mary, whose obsession with uniforms cannot be over-emphasised. She knew that the only way for a woman to claim the sort of power and authority held by men was to dress in clothes which were distinctly un-feminine and militaristic. But it was also her personal choice to dress as much as possible like a man. Judith Halberstam identifies the underlying personal reasons for wearing uniforms that made the wearer look more like a man than a woman:

> Before the mid-1920s the only way a middle-class woman stood any chance of wearing clothes which were not feminine, let alone trousers, was by wearing a uniform. Belonging to an organization such as the WPS which required members to wear a military-style uniform gave to the

watching heterosexual world a justification of why a woman was wearing men's clothes.[4]

The Metropolitan Police, fearing Mary's growing influence as a recognised policewoman, found the only point of attack to be her uniform, which explains why they were willing to go to the lengths of prosecuting the WAS for masquerading as Metropolitan policewomen.

There can be little doubt that a degree of distaste for female homosexuality underlay attempts by the Metropolitan Police to undermine and discredit the WAS. Repeated attempts were made in the 1920s to outlaw lesbianism, often by men who had no understanding of it. In a Commons Amendment in 1921, the Lord Chancellor asserted that, 'of every thousand women, taken as a whole, 999 have never even heard a whisper of these practices'.[5] Frederick MacQuisten MP believed it to be 'a matter for medical science and for neurologists'; and Ernest Wild stated that, 'it would be difficult to recite the various forms of malpractices between women ... we do not want to pollute the House with details of these abominations. This vice does exist and it saps the fundamental institutions of society. In the first place, it stops child-birth.'[6]

Women, on the other hand, whatever their sexual orientation, tended to admire Mary, and found her gentle and kind; at least, those who knew her personally and had no political axes to grind. A New Zealander, Bessie Spencer, left for London in 1916 to undertake war work, where she met Mary at the WPS headquarters: 'a very striking and attractive personality. Tall, broad, somewhat thickset, a wide, strong face, full of vigour and kindliness ... most smart and capable in her neat blue uniform. One feels she is a force.'[7]

Mary was lampooned for her appearance in a novel by C.S. Lewis. A character called 'Fairy' Hardcastle 'had been at different times a suffragette, a pacifist, and a British Fascist. She had been manhandled by the police and imprisoned. On the other hand, she had met Prime Ministers, Dictators, and famous film stars.'[8] She is both attractive and repellent to the novel's protagonist, Mark Studdock:

> It would be misleading to say that he liked her. She had indeed excited in him all the distaste which a young man feels at the proximity of something rankly, even insolently, sexed and at the same time wholly unattractive. And something in her cold eye had told him that she was well aware of this reaction and found it amusing.

No doubt Mary took this in good part. She may even have been flattered by the attention.

❧ ❧

Helen Bourn Tagart (known to her family as Ellie, but as Helen to Mary) was born at Parkfield, a sizeable mansion in Bath in 1876, the daughter of William Henry Tagart and Anna Maria Tagart (*née* Peters, and daughter of Samuel Peters, a wealthy American). Helen had one sister and two brothers. She was educated at Bath High School and the Musical International College, and was an accomplished pianist. She inherited large amounts of money from her mother and her aunt, but her estate on her death amounted to comparatively little.

Helen died at the home she shared with Mary (Littlebourne Lodge, The Esplanade, Sandgate, Folkestone, Kent) of colon cancer on 7 February 1956, leaving £1,679 16s 10d gross (£416 3s 11d net) in her will. She was 79 (according to her date of birth) but her age is given as 69 on her death certificate. The informant (on the same day) was 'Mary S. Allen causing the body to be buried'. Mary had known Helen for more than thirty years, and surely knew how old she was. Helen's will had been made on 15 April 1929, when she was living at 50 Morpeth Mansions, Westminster, leaving everything to Mary, who was her sole executor. (The will, a rather untidy document, was witnessed by Janet S. Burrow and Dorothy A. Bowker. Dorothy had been a militant suffragette.) This will, followed by twenty-seven years of companionship, suggests a very close and enduring relationship. Helen travelled the world with Mary, and was photographed with her on several occasions, usually standing a step behind her, and hardly ever smiling.

Mary rarely mentions Miss Tagart, and when she does it is in an impersonal way. During her appeal hearing on 6 November 1940 she says, when asked when she saw Hitler, 'My officer would know much better than I do, because she always travels with me. She speaks the languages much better. I will get that point cleared up for you, if you like. She will remember the date.' Asked if she speaks German when in Germany, Mary says 'My officer generally does'.[9]

Her interrogator later asks: 'Who is the lady with you? Is she Miss Tagart?'

To which Mary replies: 'She is one of my officers'. This seems rather a callous attitude to a companion of so many years, but Mary's speech was generally brusque, so perhaps we should not read anything uncaring into it. Certainly Helen cared for her; when Mary was suspected of subversive activities in the 1930s, Helen wrote long and passionate letters in her defence to everyone she thought should listen.

Around the time of Helen's death in 1956, Mary Allen wrote to Helen's brother, Edward, in South Africa, asking him for money (which he refused). Her other brother, Sam, disliked Mary intensely, but went to Helen's funeral with Edward's son, Robin. The family may well have thought that Mary had helped her spend her fortune; and that, with her right-wing political views, she had led Helen astray.

Mary wrote to Edward, again in Cape Town on 26 January 1956 to tell him that Helen was seriously ill with an inoperable cancer, and that she might live for a month, or only for a few days. Mary had taken her home from hospital, where Helen had been distressed and unhappy, and engaged two nurses to help care for her. The doctor advised Mary not to tell Helen how seriously ill she was, and Mary concurred.

Edward's son, Robin, himself a doctor, visited ten days later. He wrote to his father that she was not conscious all the time, but when she was she worried how Mary would manage without her. 'She said she has had a most interesting life and has no fear at all of death. Miss Allen is very distressed by it all but is looking after Aunt Ellie kindly in her own fashion.' He described the flat where Mary and Helen lived as 'quite pleasant but, of course, not at all luxurious'. He also said that the priest visited each evening and 'I told Miss Allen on no account to be too proud to ask me for financial help if she needed it but she said she was managing at present but would let me know "when the coffers were empty"'. Robin's attitude throughout this difficult period seems to have been tolerant and not unfriendly.

Mary acknowledged this offer of financial help in a letter of 6 February to Edward, in which she said that Helen was now unconscious, and the funeral would be in Hythe. 'She will be in the Church all night before Mass is said.'

Robert went to the funeral with Sam, and reported to his father that 'everyone behaved with dignity although Sam can't stand Miss Allen'. He questions the fact that Helen left all the family things to Mary, as stipulated in her will, and he wonders if it is worth enquiring about the existence of another will.

Towards the end of February, Mary wrote a somewhat incoherent letter to Edward, telling him that she had injured her hand (presumably to explain why she had not been able to go through Helen's possessions, as he had requested) and appealing for funds to pay nursing and funeral expenses. At the same time, she complained unwisely that Sam's remarks had been unsympathetic: 'To find a friend after thirty years of living with one you love is not possible, so I am alone here'. Edward replied, refusing to give Mary any money, but expressing gratitude for all she had done for Helen.

Sam wrote to Edward in March: 'I'm thankful it was you and not I, at the receiving end of Allen's impudent "try on".' He complains about Mary keeping valuables that he feels he should have inherited:

> How A. [Allen] can even drag in cost of laundry, telephones etc. incurred on account of her alleged 'beloved friend' passes my understanding … I felt extremely resentful at her arranging the time of the funeral and the wording of the obituary notice without consulting any of us before it was too late to alter because I had a strong suspicion that the trip over the carpet was a whisky tumbler … However I've no intention of wrangling with Allen about it. Its all too sick-making.

The offending obituary notice reads:

> TAGART – On Feb. 7, at Littlebourne Lodge, Sandgate, Kent, HELEN BOURN TAGART, beloved friend and loyal colleague of Mary S. Allen OBE. Fortified by the Rites of Holy Church. Requiem Mass at Hythe Catholic Church on Friday, Feb. 10, at 11 am followed by interment at Hythe Cemetery. Flowers to Hambrook and Johns, 1 Dymchurch Road, Hythe.

Mary replied:

> There is nothing I can say except express surprise. Your last letter offered help with expenses – and now a blank refusal … I can but say that Helen's loss has taken away all joy in life, and what I think of those who came near and joined in her last rites, and who quite obviously thought of other things and then wrote to you, will take me a long time to recover from.

Mary also wrote to someone called Muriel, apparently in response to a request for 'the return of a small box'. Muriel wrote on the back of Mary's letter: 'I received this last week – an answer to my letter I told you of, at last, and only because I wrote an urgent note requesting back the rubber cushion I had lent Ellie when she was dying … Please spit on letter and then burn it!'

It seems that unfriendliness on the part of Helen's brothers quickly turned to outright hostility. In a postscript to his letter to Edward, Sam writes, 'Allen writes on some of the quite expensive writing paper I sent Ellie at Xmas time; I expect since poor Ellie became ill soon after Xmas A. finished up the Burgundy and cigarettes!' This is particularly harsh, and can only be explained by the family's belief that Mary was holding on to items they thought should be returned to them.

An enduring mystery is how Mary financed her life. When she left home, her father made her an allowance, although how much he gave her is unknown. When he died three years later, in 1911, he left everything to his wife, Margaret (£1,987 net). Margaret Damer Dawson left everything to Mary in her will, but by the time she died the net value of that estate was nil. Mary continued to live at Danehill, Margaret's house, so presumably the ownership was transferred to her. We do not know the contents of Mary's mother's will (she died in 1933); but in 1940, Mary claimed that she owned three houses on the south coast.[10] Helen Tagart's will left Mary a net value of £416 3s 11d when she died in 1958, and Mary herself left a gross estate of some £289, net value nil.

Margaret Damer Dawson and Helen Bourn Tagart were extremely wealthy women. We can only assume that Mary lived extravagantly at their expense.

Mary Sophia Allen died on 16 December 1964 at Birdhurst Nursing Home, Croydon. She was 86 – a grand age for someone who had been a frail child, not expected to have a long life, protected from too much exercise, whose health was later compromised by imprisonment and force-feeding. The cause of death on the death certificate is cerebral thrombosis and cerebral arteriosclerosis, which suggests a series of strokes. Her occupation is given as 'Commandant, Women's Police Force – retired'.

Mary's funeral mass was celebrated on 23 December 1964 at St Gertrude's Church, conducted by Father P. Taggart (Mary had converted to Roman Catholicism in 1953, being received into the church at Hythe Catholic Church),[11] followed by burial at Greenlawn Memorial Park in Warlingham, where a simple plaque reads: 'In loving memory of Mary Sophia Allen OBE died December 1964. RIP.' The funeral directors, Messrs Shakespeares, provided one car for the funeral.

Her will, made at 17 Grimston Gardens, Folkestone and dated 14 April 1958, leaves everything to her sister, Alice Christine Sandeman (Christine).

The gross value of the will was £289 1s 0d, and the net value nil. Christine was present at the funeral.

An obituary in *The Times* (18 December 1964) gives a brief outline of her life, and mentions her support for Hitler and Franco. It is accompanied by an unflattering photograph of Mary in uniform, in which she is smiling broadly from a somewhat bloated face.

✿✿✿

Looking back over her life it is hard to decide whether Mary Allen was mad or bad; or both. She was a woman of contradictions: warm and loving to her friends, but hated by her enemies. For all her obsessions, follies and misdeeds, she earns at least some praise for her unflagging energy and loyalty, even if they were sometimes misplaced. She would be proud to be remembered in this biography, but would no doubt say that such a memorial was no more than she deserved.

Appendix I

Mary Allen's 'Call to Women' Issued in November 1933

WOMEN'S RESERVE

FOR

GOD, KING AND COUNTRY

For those of us to whom the defence of our King and Country is a sacred trust, the appeal to women to enrol for service is no alarmist cry, but one which all should be proud to answer. The ideals and traditions of the British Empire are a vital force for good to the whole world and it is for us to consider seriously whether at this time the need for a more active expression of our loyalty is not demanded. Many are absorbing subversive teachings, not realising that the steady undermining of the 'Will to serve' is the ultimate aim of the enemies in our midst. Ours is no call to prepare for war; it is, on the contrary, one to prepare all women to be in a position to ensure peace and to be strong enough to counteract and deal with danger from whatever source it may come. Those who call on men and women to strike in the event of any action being taken by the Government with which they do not agree, are the 'alarmists' of the present day, not those who, realising the immense strides subversive propaganda is making, are not prepared to allow it to proceed unchallenged.

The unreadiness of those who advocate a negative attitude is our greatest danger. Our freedom is being challenged on every side, by the incitement of masses of our countrymen and women to render any action taken by the authorities abortive and interfere in such a manner with the forces of law and order that industry is held up and our ultimate security imperilled. The desire to serve and the capacity to face the truth clear-eyed and steadfast is as great as ever, and women by volunteering for service have in their hands a weapon which will not only be a deterrent to all subversive forces, but which can be instrumental in counteracting the poisonous doctrines accepted now as part of the freedom of speech movement, frequently masquerading under the banner of peace. At each successive onslaught we should be ready calmly and quietly to state that, whether in peace or war, we are willing and able to uphold the ideals of those who made our Empire. No longer must we countenance the gradual weakening of our faith in patriotism nor the fear that, if we organise and train ourselves for future emergency, we shall be spoken of as preparing for war. Our aim is so to be ready that, whenever and wherever we are needed, we shall be competent and worthy to answer the call and ready to carry out the duties which devolve on us as women.

May the response be so great that those who seek to bring this country under the control of disruptive forces may realise the futility of their efforts.

'If God is for us, who can prevail against us?'

MARY S. ALLEN
Commandant

Appendix II

REPORT ON THE SEARCH ON 10 JULY 1940 OF MARY'S HOME

Cornwall Constabulary
Secret

Sir,

<u>Mary ALLAN [*sic*] Nanquidno Valley, St Just</u>
With reference to Home Office letter of the 15th instant, Ref. No. 512110/26, I respectfully report that at 4 pm on Tuesday, 16.7.40, I visited Miss Allan's residence at Nanquidno Valley, St Just, in company with Det/Con. Roberts and Sergeant Penhaligon.

I served copies of the Detention Order and Suspension Order on Miss Allan and informed her that it is open to her to make objections against the Detention Order, and to any of the conditions attached to the Suspension Order, and supplied her with the name and address of the Secretary, Home Office Advisory Committee, 6 Burlington Gardens W1. I also informed her that she could make representations to the Secretary of State if she so desired.

Miss Allan's residence at Nanquidno Valley is situate in a very lonely spot and is reached by a very rough and muddy lane. It is about 3 miles from the nearest shops which are either at St Just or Sennen. On reading the conditions of the Suspension Order Miss Allan stated she would object, and stated that she could not notify her movements weekly to the officer in charge at the nearest Police Station at St Just because she was unable to walk there owing to an injured knee. I informed her that if she could not walk she would have no movements to report.

Her car is kept in a garage about 300 yards from the house. She immediately telephoned to an engineer at St Just, informed him that she was not [*sic*] longer allowed to use her car and requested that he call, jack the car up on blocks, take away the batteries and rotor arm, lock up the garage and hand the key to Sergeant Penhaligon at the Police Station, St Just.

At 5.40 pm she telephoned the St Just telephone Exchange informed the operator that she was no longer allowed to have the use of a telephone and gave instructions that from then onwards her telephone was to be cut off, that no calls were to be put through to her and that she could not make any calls. I later called at the GPO, Penzance, where I saw Mr A.H. Wardrop, Overseer in Charge. I informed him that by order of the Secretary of State Miss Allan's telephone must be disconnected. He immediately telephoned the St Just exchange and verified that Miss Allan's telephone had been closed since 5.40 pm, and stated he would make arrangements for Engineers to disconnect the telephone in Miss Allan's house.

I took possession of three portable Wireless Receiving Sets and these are now at Camborne Police Station.

Miss Allan's house was searched and I took possession of the following articles, viz:-

Two Membership Cards of the British Union of Fascists issued to Commandant Mary S. ALLAN, Danehill, Lympne, Kent.
Two Membership Cards of the British Union of Fascists issued to Miss Helen Bourn TAGART, Danehill, Lympne, Kent. (Miss Tagart is Miss Allan's Companion Secretary and resides with Miss Allan at Nanquidno Valley, St Just.)
Publications of 'ACTION' dated 18.4.40, 25.4.40, 2.5.40, 9.5.40, 16.5.40, 23.5.40, 30.5.40 (3 copies), and 6.6.40. In five of these publications Miss Allan wrote articles on 'End this Indecency' 'Refugees and Vice' 'Indecent Photographs' 'Nude Exhibitionism' and 'Women's Responsibilities'.
Letter dated 5th July 1940, from Miss Elizabeth Vavasour, 29 Hatherley Road, Sidcup, Kent, asking if Miss Allan could let her have the articles which she wrote in 'ACTION'
Letter dated 5th July 1940, from Miss Elizabeth Vavasour, 29 Hatherley Road, Sidcup, Kent, again endeavouring to obtain copies of the articles written by Miss Allan in 'Action'.
'Gentile Folly: the Rothschilds' a 1s 0d anti-Jewish Book by Arnold Leese.
Pamphlet headed 'The Plan of the Jew!'
Pamphlet head 'Federal Union. Jewish Slave State to end Nationalism. The Plan revealed'.

Newspaper Cuttings, and the 'Daily Mail' dated 13.6.40, containing an article, re Miss Mary Allan being a Fascist, and question being asked concerning her in the House of Parliament.

The above mentioned articles are in my possession at this Station.

I enclose copies of the letters written by Miss Elizabeth Vavasour, referred to above, but as the articles written by Miss Allan appear to have little or no political significance, it would appear that Miss Vavasour's request to have copies of the articles are more for social reform reasons that for political purposes.

Both Miss Mary Allan and her Secretary, Miss Taggart [*sic*], declined to express any opinions concerning their views of the International Situation. They both joined the British Union of Fascists on 6.12.39, and Miss Taggart stated they joined the British Union because they wanted Britain for the British, and Miss Mary Allan had lectured a British Union Meeting on a 'Negotiated Peace' but this was some time ago.

Endorsed copies of the Detention and Suspension Order served on Miss Mary Allan are respectfully attached.

I am, Sir, Your obedient Servant,
(SGD.) PERCIVAL G. MARTIN
Act. Det/Sergeant

Sir, Respectfully submitted.
(SGD.) E. W. Morish
Superintendent.

REFERENCES AND NOTES

LIB = *Lady in Blue*
PP = *The Pioneer Policewoman*
WXR = *A Woman at the Cross Roads*

Chapter 1

1   Mary S. Allen and Julie H. Heyneman (1934) *A Woman at the Cross Roads*, London: Unicorn, p.14.
2   Mary S. Allen and Julie H. Heyneman (1925) *The Pioneer Policewoman*, London: Chatto & Windus, p.16.
3   Donald Clark (1991) *A Daisy in the Broom: the story of a school, 1820–1958*, Broughton in Tweeddale, p.282.
4   *Great Western Railway Magazine*, December 1903, Vol. XV, No.12.
5   Patrick Benham (2006) *The Avalonians*, Somerset: Gothic Image Publications, p.59.
6   Bunty Martin, letter to Patrick Benham, 24 March 1988.
7   Bunty Martin, *ibid*.
8   David Hilliard (1982) *Unenglish and Unmanly*, Indiana University Press, http://anglicanhistory.org/academic/hilliard_unenglish.pdf, accessed 22 February 2012.
9   Peter F. Anson (1958) *Abbot Extraordinary: A Memoir of Aelred Carlyle, Monk and Missionary, 1874–1955*, London: Faith Press.
10 For a more complete biography of Aelred Carlyle, see Rene Kollar (2003) *Travels in America: Aelred Carlyle, his American "Allies", and Anglican Benedictine Monasticism*.
11 Bunty Martin, letter to Patrick Benham, 9 May 1988.
12 Bunty Martin, *ibid*.
13 National Archives, FO383/333/C358353.
14 Patrick Benham, *op. cit*.
15 Gerry Fenge (2010) *The Two Worlds of Wellesley Tudor Pole*, Starseed Publications.
16 Gerry Fenge, *op. cit*.
17 Patrick Benham, personal communication, 31 December 2008.
18 Gerry Fenge, *op. cit*.
19 Patrick Benham, *op. cit*. p.131, quoting from *Stanbrook Abbey House Chronicle*.
20 Bunty Martin, 24 March 1988.
21 Bunty Martin, 9 May 1988.
22 Bunty Martin, 24 March 1988.
23 Patrick Benham, *op. cit*., p.123.
24 Bunty Martin, 24 March 1988.
25 Bunty Martin, *ibid*.

Chapter 2
1 Mary Allen (1936) *Lady in Blue*, London: Stanley Paul, pp.13–14.
2 Emmeline Pethick Lawrence (1938) *My Part in a Changing World*, London, p.151.
3 Sylvia Pankhurst (1977, first published 1931) *The Suffragette Movement*, p.185.
4 LIB, p.13.
5 LIB, p.15.
6 Christabel Pankhurst (1959) *Unshackled: the story of how we won the vote*, London: Hutchinson, p.43.
7 Martin Pugh (2002) *The Pankhursts*, London: Penguin, pp.50–51.
8 *The Observer*, 6 December 1908, p.9.
9 Brian Harrison, 'The Act of Militancy: Violence and the Suffragettes, 1904–1914', in Michael Bentley and John Stevenson (eds) (1982) *Peaceable Kingdom: Stability and Change in Modern Britain*, Oxford: Oxford University Press, pp.80–122.

Chapter 3
1 LIB, p.15.
2 LIB, p.16.
3 LIB, p.19.
4 WXR, p.59.
5 Antonia Raeburn (1973) *The Militant Suffragettes*, London: Michael Joseph Ltd, p.110.
6 Dobbie, B.M. Willmott (1979) *A Nest of Suffragettes in Somerset*, Bath: The Batheaston Society, p.34.
7 *The Times*, 15 November 1909, p.14.
8 *A Nest of Suffragettes in Somerset*, p.38.
9 WXR, p.59.
10 LIB, pp.21–22.
11 Margaret Bateman, personal communication, 7 January 2009.

Chapter 4
1 LIB, p.19.
2 *Daily Telegraph*, 18 February 1908.
3 June Purvis (1995) 'The prison experiences of suffragettes in Edwardian Britain', *Women's History Review*, 4:1, 103–133, pp.122–3.
4 Dodge and Forward, *op. cit.*, p.801.
5 Hansard, 7 November 1906.
6 Hansard, 18 February 1908.
7 Antonia Raeburn (1973) *The Militant Suffragettes*, London: Michael Joseph Ltd, p.113.
8 LIB, p.22.
9 *Votes for Women*, 23 February 1912.
10 LIB, p.23.
11 Christabel Pankhurst, letter to Janie Allan, 6 May 1914.
12 Christabel Pankhurst, letter to Janie Allan, 26 May 1914.
13 Quoted in Krista Cowman (2007) *Women of the Right Spirit*, Manchester University Press p.149.
14 June Purvis, 'Deeds, not words: the daily lives of militant suffragettes in Edwardian Britain', *Women's Studies International Forum*, 1995, 18, 2 , p.96.
15 June Purvis, 'Deeds, not words': the daily lives of militant suffragettes in Edwardian Britain', p.100.
16 *Britannia's Glory*, pp.20–1.
17 *The Pankhursts, op. cit.*, p.94.

18 LIB, pp.17–18.
19 Crawford, p.9.
20 Helena Wojtczak, *Women of 19th Century Hastings and St Leonards.*
21 LIB, p.24.
22 LIB, p.25.

Chapter 5
1 LIB, p.25.
2 WXR, p.67.
3 LIB, p.25; WXR, p.67.
4 *Policewoman's Review*, VII, 8 December 1933.
5 PP, p.9.
6 http://www.metwpa.org.uk/viewpage.php?page.
7 *Report of the Women Police Service 1918–19*, Imperial War Museum, EMP43/95.
8 PP, p.18.
9 PP, pp.12–13.
10 *Votes for Women*, 29 May 1914.
11 *The Times*, 11 October 1916.
12 *Votes for Women*, 4 June 1915.
13 PP, pp.18–19.
14 LIB, p.28.
15 *Report 1918–19*, p.8.
16 LIB, p.19.
17 LIB, p.28.
18 PP, p.21.
19 *Report 1918–19*, p.3.
20 *The Times*, 2 April 1930.
21 PP, p.25.
22 Alison J. Laurie (2003) *Lady-Husbands and Kamp Ladies: pre-1970 Lesbian Life in Aotearoa/New Zealand*, PhD Thesis, Victoria University of Wellington, pp.195–96.
23 Emily Hamer (1996) *Britannia's Glory*, London: Cassell, pp.46–7.

Chapter 6
1 LIB, p.27.
2 PP, p.28.
3 PP, p.30.
4 LIB, p.31.
5 PP, p.31.
6 PP, p.33.
7 PP, p.34.
8 *Feminist Freikorps*, p.37 and note 21.
9 PP, p.34.
10 PP, p.35.
11 LIB, p.32.
12 *Report 1918–19*, p.5; PP, p.38.
13 PP, p.42.
14 PP, p.44.
15 LIB, p.35.
16 PP, p.46.
17 PP, p.48.

18 LIB, p.22.
19 PP, p.48.
20 Bunty Martin, 24 March 1988.
21 PP, p.56.
22 LIB, p.40.
23 PP, pp.56–7.
24 *Ibid.*, p.66.
25 LIB, p.37.
26 PP, p.268.
27 PP, p.73.
28 WXR, p.77.
29 Angela Woollacott (1994) *On Her their Lives Depend: Munition Workers in the Great War*, London: University of California Press, p.166.
30 PP, p.100.
31 PP, p.101.
32 PP, p.101.
33 http://www.britishpathe.com/record.php?id=78690 accessed 6 August 2009.

Chapter 7
1 LIB, p.46–8.
2 LIB, p.48.
3 LIB, p.48.
4 *Daily Mail*, 3 October 1918.
5 Joan Lock (1979) *The British Policewoman: Her Story*, London: Robert Hale Ltd, p.89.
6 *The Times*, 22 December 1919.
7 *Ibid.*
8 LIB, p.50.
9 PRO HO 45 11067.
10 Pioneer, p.85.
11 Laura Doan (2001) *Fashioning Sapphism: the origins of modern English lesbian culture*, Columbia University Press.
12 LIB, p.50.
13 *The Times*, 25 May 1920.
14 PP, p.173.
15 Pioneer, p.174.
16 *The Times*, 8 March 1921.
17 *The Times*, 17 March 1921.
18 *The Times*, 22 March 1921.
19 *The Times*, 13 May 1921.
20 *The Times*, 30 August 1922.
21 *The Times*, 1 September 1922.
22 *The Times*, 3 November 1922.
23 WXR, p.106.

Chapter 8
1 LIB, p.54.
2 LIB, p.55.
3 *Pioneer Policewoman*, p.22.
4 LIB, p.62.
5 LIB, p.63.

6 *Pioneer Policewoman*, p.202.
7 *Ibid.*, p.203.
8 *Pioneer Policewoman*, p.203.
9 *Ibid.*, p.207.
10 Joan Lock, p.149.
11 LIB, p.67.
12 PP, p.214.
13 LIB, pp.72–3.
14 *New York Times*, 27 April 1924.
15 LIB, p.75.
16 PP, p.215.
17 LIB, p.76.
18 LIB, pp.77–8.
19 PP, p.220.
20 LIB, p.80.
21 *Toronto Daily Star*, 15 May 1924.
22 http://www.britishpathe.com/video/english-police-women-in-canada.
23 LIB, p.81.
24 LIB, p.83.
25 LIB, p.84.
26 LIB, p.85.
27 PP, p.221.
28 PP, p.210.
29 LIB, p.90.
30 LIB, p.86.
31 *Flight*, 31 May 1928 and 14 June 1928.
32 *Flight*, 24 November 1932.

Chapter 9

1 LIB, p.93.
2 LIB, p.94.
3 *The Times*, 12 May 1926.
4 LIB, p.94.
5 LIB, p.96.
6 LIB, p.97.
7 Public Record Office (PRO) HO144/21933/2.
8 PRO HO144/21933/5.
9 PRO HO144/21933/6.
10 PRO HO144/21933/7.
11 PRO HO144/21933/2.
12 *The Times*, Friday, 19 October 1928.
13 PRO HO144/21933/16.
14 PRO HO144/21933/12.
15 *The Times*, 14 March 1931.
16 *The Times*, 17 March 1931.
17 Mrs Green-Armytage was one of Janet Allen's supporters when she took her Solemn Perpetual vows in 1926.
18 *The Times*, 20 March 1931.
19 PRO HO144/21933/21.
20 PRO HO144/21933/23.

21 PRO HO144/21933/31.
22 PRO HO144/21933/30.
23 PRO HO144/21933/40.
24 PRO HO144/21933/48.
25 PRO HO144/21933/35.
26 PRO HO144/21933/32.

Chapter 10

1 Teresa Billington-Greig, 'The Truth about White Slavery', *English Review*, 14, 1913, pp.428–6.
2 Hansard, 24 July 1929.
3 LIB, p.114.
4 Mary's account differs from that given by Prof. Yunan Labib Rizk of the *Al-Ahram* History Studies Centre, who states that 'six British policewomen had arrived in Alexandria and took up duties there, with "initial results that inspire confidence" … seven years earlier there had been two women in the force: Miss Julia George of Britain at a monthly salary of LE21 and Miss Fortina from Italy at LE 18 per month.' 'Women Police', http://weekly.ahram.org.eg/2002/602/chrncls.htm, accessed 30 June 2009. This statement has not been verified.
5 LIB, p.115.
6 *Al-Ahram*, 12 February 1930.
7 'Women Police', http://weekly.ahram.org.eg/2002/602/chrncls.htm, accessed 30 June 2009.
8 *L'Egyptienne*, November 1929, year 5, No.51, translated from French by John Bosley.
9 *The Times*, 20 September 1909.
10 LIB, p.116.
11 *Policewoman's Review*, III, 36, 286.
12 *Policewoman's Review*, III, 36, April 1930.
13 *Policewoman's Review*, IV, 46, February 1931.
14 http://inspectorates.homeoffice.gov.uk/hmic/docs/about-us/history/history-partb.pdf?view=Binary, accessed 24 June 2009.
15 LIB, pp.120–1.
16 LIB, p.121.
17 LIB, pp.164–5.
18 http://inspectorates.homeoffice.gov.uk/hmic/docs/about-us/history/history-partb.pdf?view=Binary, accessed 24 June 2009.

Chapter 11

1 *Policewoman's Review*, II, 17 September 1928.
2 *Policewoman's Review*, II, 20 December 1928.
3 *Policewoman's Review*, III, 25 May 1929.
4 *Policewoman's Review*, VII, 2 June 1933.
5 *Policewoman's Review*, V, 10 February 1932.
6 New York: E.P. Dutton & Co. Inc., translated by W.D. Robson-Scott, p.320.
7 'Flying for Women', *Good Housekeeping*, August 1930.

Chapter 12

1 *The Times*, 30 October 1933.
2 LIB, p.270.

3   LIB, p.271.
4   *British Journal of Nursing*, December 1933, p.349.
5   R.M. Douglas (1999) *Feminist Freikorps: The British Voluntary Women Police, 1914–1940*, Prager, p.122.
6   HO, p.55.
7   *Ibid.*, p.57.
8   *Ibid.*, p.100.
9   *Ibid.*, p.156.
10 *Ibid.*, p.94.
11 *Ibid.*, p.219.
12 http://www.britishpathe.com/video/new-womens-reserve/query/new+womens+reserve.
13 1938, George G. Harrap & Co. Ltd.
14 *Flight*, 7 December 1933.
15 Dorril, p.22.

Chapter 13

1   LIB, p.92.
2   PP, p.200.
3   LIB, p.91.
4   LIB, p.148.
5   LIB, p.148.
6   LIB, 153.
7   PP, p.174.
8   *Glasgow Herald*, 7 April 1925.
9   PRO HO144/21933/4.
10 *British Journal of Nursing*, 20 July 1918.
11 *The Blackshirt*, 29 June 1934, p.3.
12 PRO HO144/21933/23.
13 PRO HO144/21933/56.
14 PRO HO144/21933/219.
15 http://archive.catholicherald.co.uk/article/4th-november-1953/5/the-pioneer-policewoman.
16 *Glasgow Herald*, 18 June 1938.
17 PRO HO244.
18 PRO HO416.
19 PRO HO144/21933/307.
20 *Daily Mirror*, 26 April 1940.
21 Julie Gottlieb (2002) '"Motherly Hate": Gendering Anti-Semitism in the British Union of Fascists', *Gender and History*, 14:2, 294–320, p.308.
22 Richard C. Thurlow (1998) *Fascism in Britain*, I.B. Tauris, p.179.
23 PRO HO250–1.
24 PRO HO326.
25 PRO HO327.
26 PRO HO426.
27 PRO HO254.
28 PRO HO252.
29 Hansard, *HC Deb*, 27 June 1940, Vol.362, cc583.

Chapter 14

1 PRO HO405.
2 PRO HO410.
3 PRO HO411.
4 PRO HO414.
5 PRO HO428–30.
6 PRO HO622–23.
7 PRO HO641.
8 PRO HO647.
9 PRO HO615.
10 PRO HO553.
11 PRO HO557–59.

Chapter 15

1 PRO HO144/21933/21.
2 Michael Baker (1985) *Our three Selves: a life of Radclyffe Hall*, Hamish Hamilton, p.267.
3 *Ibid.*, p.274.
4 Judith Halberstam (1998) *Female Masculinity*, Durham and London, Duke University Press, pp.107–8.
5 HL Debate, 15 August 1921, Vol.43 c 574.
6 Hansard, 4 August 1921, p.1801.
7 Alison J. Laurie (2003) *Lady-husbands and kamp ladies*, Victoria University of Wellington doctoral thesis, pp.195–6.
8 *That Hideous Strength*, London: Bodley Head (1945), p.80; I am grateful to Paul Ashdown for pointing out this connection.
9 PRO HO411,415.
10 PRO HO144/21933/391.
11 *Catholic Herald*, 4 November 1953.

INDEX

Visit our website and discover thousands of
other History Press books.

www.thehistorypress.co.uk